FIXER-UPPER

THE RUSSO SISTERS, BOOK 3

LINDA SEED

GET A LINDA SEED SHORT STORY FREE

Sign up for Linda's no-spam newsletter and get a free copy of the Main Street Merchants short story "Jacks Are Wild" and more exclusive content at no cost.

Subscribe at www.lindaseed.com.

This is a work of fiction. Any characters, organizations, places, or events portrayed in this novel are either products of the author's imagination or are used fictitiously.

FIXER-UPPER
Copyright © 2019 by Linda Seed

ISBN: 978-1-7343453-0-8

The author is available for book signings, book club discussions, conferences, and other appearances.
Linda Seed may be contacted via e-mail at linda@lindaseed.com or on Facebook at www.facebook.com/LindaSeedAuthor. Learn more about Linda Seed's novels at www.lindaseed.com.

Cover design by Teaberry Creative.

BY LINDA SEED

1

—————

"Ooh. Look at this bear claw." Benedetta Russo waved a sugary, buttery pastry in front of her sister Martina, taunting her. "You know you want one. Smell it. Cinnamon and brown sugar! Oh, the soft, wholesome goodness."

"There's nothing wholesome about refined sugar." Martina smiled serenely. "But if you want to put momentary gratification over your health—"

"I do. I really do." Benny took a bite of the pastry and moaned with pleasure. "Oh, God. This is amazing."

The four Russo sisters didn't usually make time to have breakfast together, even though three of them lived in the same house. Most mornings, they all scrambled to make coffee, grab whatever nourishment was handy, and get out the door to their various jobs.

But Sofia's wedding was just four months away, and a lot still needed to be done. That called for a family meeting. Through a series of phone calls, texts, and in-person conversations, they'd determined that the only time they could all be available was on a Tuesday morning at seven a.m.

So here they were, in the big living room of the renovated log cabin that Sofia, Martina, and Benny shared. Bianca, as the one sister who didn't live there and who, therefore, had to be out in her car anyway, had brought a box of bear claws and croissants from the French Corner Bakery.

Benny had made a big pot of coffee, and three of the sisters were sitting on the sofa with steaming, fragrant mugs of French roast, plates of pastries balanced on their laps.

Martina, as usual, was sipping a mug of herbal tea in place of the coffee. Instead of a pastry, she was eating a breakfast of Greek yogurt, homemade granola, and organic pears she'd bought at the farmer's market.

"Speaking of health." Sofia eyed the coffee mug sitting on the table in front of Bianca, who was six months pregnant and whose midsection bulged beneath her T-shirt. "Should you be drinking that?"

"I'm a doctor." Bianca eyed her sister sternly. "Are you giving me medical advice?"

"Well ..."

"There is no credible evidence—none—showing that one cup of coffee a day is detrimental to a developing fetus. I'm bloated, I can't drink alcohol, my clothes don't fit anymore, and I'm not sleeping because I have to get up twice a night to pee. I need this coffee. It's the one thing saving my sanity. Do you want to take my sanity away, Sofia? Do you?"

Bianca stared down her sister, who put up her hands in surrender. "No. Of course not. Drink up."

"You know, there are some herbal blends I can recommend that will help with sleep. And with mood," Martina said.

"My mood's fine!" Bianca snapped. Then her shoulders fell. "Well, okay, maybe it isn't. Aside from the lack of sleep, I've got heartburn, and my ankles are the size of tree trunks."

"You know, they really are." Benny peered down at Bianca's feet.

"How's TJ holding up?" Sofia asked. Bianca's husband, so far, had been a model of manly support.

"He's doing his best to deal with my hormones," Bianca said. "Last night, I cried because he cut my sandwich in half down the middle instead of diagonally."

"Owen must be excited though, right?" Sofia asked. Owen was TJ's teenage son from a previous marriage.

Bianca smiled fondly. "Yeah. He's already bought a gift for the baby. A stuffed bunny. He's so sweet. He can't wait to be a big brother."

They chatted a little longer about this and that, and then Martina said, "Okay, should we get to it?"

She didn't have to be anywhere for a while—she ran her interior design business out of her home, and she didn't have any client meetings until ten. But the others were on tighter schedules. Bianca and Sofia had to open Bianca's pediatrics office at nine, and Benny, a marine biologist, was teaching a class at the community college in San Luis Obispo at eight thirty. If they spent all morning talking about Bianca's dietary habits and hormonal fluctuations, they wouldn't get anything done.

"Yes, let's." Sofia pulled out a thick three-ring binder, opened it to a page of notes about the wedding, and uncapped a pen. They'd all been assigned different tasks to prepare for the ceremony, the reception, and the various events surrounding them, and they hadn't touched base in a while on where they all stood. "I need status reports. Flowers?"

As Benny hunted around in her bag for the contract she'd signed for the floral arrangements, Martina tried to drum up some enthusiasm. It was going to be a beautiful wedding, and Sofia would be a stunning bride with her perfect figure, glossy hair, and olive-toned skin. Sofia's fiancé, Patrick, was going to be struck speechless when she walked down the aisle.

It had been hard to get Sofia to this point, to get her past her grief over their parents—or, at least, far enough past it that she could let herself be happy.

There was no way Martina was going to ruin all of that progress by being jealous of Sofia's happiness—or of Bianca's.

She was happy for her sisters, she really was. Despite Bianca's complaints about her ankles and her hormones, she was glowing, not only with the anticipation of motherhood, but also with love for her new husband and stepson.

Things were falling into place for Martina's sisters. She just couldn't help wondering when they would fall into place for her, too.

Martina's business, launched just a few years ago, was doing well in some ways. One of her projects had been featured on the cover of this month's *Central Coast Home* magazine. But she'd suffered a setback when one of her clients had refused to make his final payment, claiming that a broken pipe in the kitchen—something Martina and her contractor had nothing to do with—had been her fault.

Martina knew she could win in court, but the cost of a lawyer—not to mention the time she'd lose dealing with the whole mess—made her uncertain whether she wanted to deal with it.

And that meant her goal of buying a fixer-upper for herself and turning it into the house of her dreams was that much further away.

Martina loved living with her sisters in the house they'd inherited from their parents. The cabin, a former whorehouse that Aldo and Carmela had remodeled themselves, had been a lifeline for Martina when her parents had died. Everything about the house, from its heavy beams to its oak floors to its hand-carved doorknobs, brought back memories of her mother and father, making her feel that, in a way, they'd never really gone.

That had been so important in the days and months after their deaths, when it had been all Martina could do to keep functioning, keep breathing. But the house was their vision, their labor of love, not hers. She had her own vision, one she finally felt she was ready to pursue—if she ever had the money.

She hoped that when it finally happened, she'd have a family of her own to share it with.

When Martina had moved back home to Cambria, California, to be with her sisters after her mother's cancer and her father's accident, she hadn't realized how small the dating pool was here. The town only had about six thousand residents to begin with, and many were retirees. Sometimes she worried that Bianca and Sofia had snagged the last eligible men in their age range, leaving no one for her.

Martina was still musing about all of that when she realized Sofia was talking to her.

" ... bachelorette party. Martina?"

Martina looked up. "What?"

"What's the status on the bachelorette party?" Sofia repeated.

"Oh. Sorry. We're going to have drinks at Ted's. Pool, darts, et cetera. We'll assign designated drivers to get everyone home. Which brings us to an important question. Strippers, or no strippers?"

CHRISTOPHER MILLS DIDN'T WANT to fight with his girlfriend. In fact, he would have preferred to have his spleen pulled out through his ear. And yet, it seemed like fighting with Alexis took up most of his time since they'd moved to Cambria.

Right now, they were fighting about the house. Cooper House, a twenty-two-room Victorian mansion built in the late 1800s by logging tycoon Eustace Cooper, was a disappointment to Chris's girlfriend on many levels.

The rooms were too dark. The downstairs was too cold, and the upstairs was too hot. The décor wasn't modern enough. And the property, set back from the coast in the hills above Cambria, had an inadequate ocean view, in Alexis's opinion. Yes, you could see the Pacific from the pool, but most of the living areas offered barely a glimpse of blue through the trees. What was the point of having a high-end home in a beach town if you didn't have an unobstructed view of the coastline?

"Alexis." Chris rubbed his eyes with his fingertips, already weary even though the day had barely started. "I know you didn't want to move here. I'm aware that you did it for me. But could you maybe *try* not to focus on the negative?"

The fact was, he liked Cooper House. Liked its imposing silhouette, liked the solid sound the floors made when you walked on them, liked the echo of its ceilings and the mood of its dark-paneled library.

He'd always liked it, even if there'd been a period of years when it had sat mostly empty and he'd barely made the time to stay here. He'd bought it as a weekend place, but with the demands of his work, those weekends had been more and more rare until he might have forgotten he owned the house if not for the regular reports from his caretaker.

Now that he'd sold his company—raking in an obscene profit in the transaction—he finally could enjoy some free, unstructured time. And this was where he wanted to enjoy it.

"I'm not *focusing* on the *negative.*" Alexis put emphasis on Chris's own words as she spat them back at him. "I'm merely pointing out some very real issues that seem to have escaped you." She allowed herself a small curve of her lips. "Not that I should be surprised. Men have such a poor sense of aesthetics."

Did they? He could have cited a long list of successful painters, sculptors, clothing designers, interior designers, and even hairstylists who, as men, could be said to have at least a rudimentary sense of aesthetics. But Alexis's voice had softened, and, for a change, she wasn't yelling at him, so he decided not to press the point.

"If it bothers you that much, why not get somebody in? Redecorate?" One thing Chris had learned about Alexis was that she was rarely angry when she was busy spending money—preferably his. If turning over his credit card to her could buy him a little peace, a little harmony, it seemed like a bargain.

"Really?" Her eyes widened in hope.

"Sure. Why not?" He went to her, put an arm around her toned waist, and pressed a kiss to her temple. "If redoing the place is going to make you more comfortable here, then you should do it."

"Jean-Claude is booked months in advance, and I'm not sure it can wait that long."

Chris refrained from pointing out that Jean-Claude, who'd done the interior design of Chris's condo in San Jose, was a man, and therefore disproved her theory about men and aesthetics.

"*Hmm.*" Chris went to the coffee table in front of the sofa, picked up a magazine, and handed it to her. "Try her." He pointed to the cover photo, which showed a sleek, modern living room with a wall of windows overlooking the ocean. The headline read, MARTINA RUSSO: ON THE CUTTING EDGE OF CENTRAL COAST DESIGN. He'd been leafing through the magazine the night before and had noticed the article.

Alexis's nose scrunched up as though she'd smelled something bad. "A local designer?" She said the word *local* as though it were synonymous with *incompetent.*

"Sure, why not? She's probably available sooner than Jean-Claude."

"Oh, well. But still ..."

"Just bring her in." If Alexis was busy interviewing designers, it would give her that much less time to find fault with him. "If you don't like her, you can still call Jean-Claude."

2

Martina got a call from Alexis Sinclair's assistant the following evening as she was looking through the refrigerator for something to make for dinner.

"Ms. Sinclair is looking for a designer for Cooper House, and she would like to meet with you as soon as possible. You are familiar with Cooper House?" The woman's voice was crisp and businesslike.

Cooper House? Of course she was familiar with Cooper House. Everyone was. She'd been dying to see the inside of it for years. And now this mystery person was calling her about actually *working* on it? "Um ... yes. Certainly. But—"

"She has availability at ten a.m. tomorrow. Is that satisfactory?"

Martina was certain she was being punked—someone she knew, possibly one of her sisters, had put someone up to this. Any minute, Sofia or Benny would pop her head around the corner and laugh, saying, *You should have seen the look on your face!*

Lacking evidence of that, though, Martina said that she was, in fact, available tomorrow at ten.

"Speak into the intercom at the security gate when you arrive, and someone will buzz you in," the woman said, then ended the call.

Who was Alexis Sinclair? Martina knew that dating app developer Christopher Mills owned Cooper House—everyone in Cambria knew that—but what did this Sinclair person have to do with him, and why did she want to see Martina?

Was it possible that Martina really might be hired to redesign Cooper House? Surely not. A job of that magnitude would be so far beyond anything she'd done before that it would be like hiring an auto mechanic to work on a 747.

"What's with you?" Benny had just walked into the room wearing a Hello Kitty T-shirt, a pair of sweatpants, and fuzzy pink slippers. Her dark hair was in two tight buns atop either side of her head, her blunt bangs falling just above her eyebrows.

"What do you mean?" Martina was still holding her cell phone.

"You look like you're about to faint. Your eyes are doing this weird pinwheel thing." Benny made a circular motion with her finger to demonstrate.

"I just ... no. It's stupid. It's not a real thing. Sofia's pranking me or something." Martina set the phone on the countertop and stared at it.

"What's stupid? What's not a real thing? And Sofia wouldn't prank you. That's more like something I would do, and I didn't."

Martina told Benny about the call from Alexis Sinclair's assistant. "Who even is Alexis Sinclair? Christopher Mills owns that house, right? I mean ... he did the last time I heard anything about it. Then this random person calls."

"*Hmm.*" Benny went to her room and came out with her laptop. She set it on the kitchen counter, opened it, and began typing. She clicked on a search result, then turned the laptop around so Martina could see the screen. "Apparently, Alexis Sinclair is Christopher Mills's squeeze. Google is your friend."

The screen displayed a blog post about a San Francisco charity auction, with bits of gossip about the couples in attendance. One photo showed Christopher Mills and a tall, shapely blond, him in a tux, her in a form-fitting, low-cut silver gown. The caption identified them as *tech mogul Christopher Mills and his latest inamorata, Alexis Sinclair.*

"Who even uses the word *inamorata* anymore?" Benny mused.

"It might actually be real," Martina said, still looking at the screen. "Alexis Sinclair. That might really have been her assistant. She and Christopher Mills might really want me to redesign Cooper House. Oh, God."

"Do you need to sit down and put your head between your knees?" Benny asked.

"Maybe." She did sit down, because her knees were feeling a bit rubbery. But once she was settled into a chair at the kitchen table, she started to feel steadier. Perhaps the head-between-the-knees thing could wait.

IN THE MORNING, Martina pondered how to prepare for the meeting. Of course, she had the portfolio, the resume, and the list of references she showed to every potential client. Was there more she should be doing? Was there some deal-clenching plan she should have in place?

She contemplated calling Bianca to borrow a business suit, then decided that was stupid. She'd be her most confident if she dressed as herself, not as some alternate, fictional person she thought they might want her to be.

Her usual style was artsy Bohemian chic, so she went with that: flowing ankle-length linen skirt, patterned blouse, sandals, a stack of bracelets on her left wrist, her hair—naturally dark brown but dyed auburn—wavy and cascading loosely down her back.

Why should she pretend she was someone she wasn't just for some rich people in a twenty-two-room mansion?

Because I really want to get my hands on that twenty-two-room mansion.

She needed a pep talk on her way out the door, but Benny was out on a boat researching sea otters, and Bianca and Sofia were at the medical practice. That left Patrick, Sofia's fiancé, who'd moved in with them earlier that year. Patrick was an English professor at Cal Poly San Luis Obispo, and he didn't have his first class until late morning.

"Tell me it's going to be okay." Martina had poked her head into Sofia and Patrick's room, where Patrick was sitting at a desk working on his laptop.

"This is the Cooper House thing, right?" He looked up from what he was doing.

"Yes. The Cooper House thing. I just need you to tell me I can do this."

"All right." His brow furrowed as he concentrated on what to say. "They wouldn't have called you if they didn't think you could handle it. People like that don't just pick somebody randomly. They researched you, and they like your work."

"Okay. This is good. Keep going."

He was warming to his topic. "You deserve this. You've worked hard, and you've earned it. And if you get this job, it's going to be because you're the best." He nodded, apparently satisfied with his speech.

"Thank you, Patrick." She rushed into the room, her messenger bag over her shoulder, and kissed his cheek. "I can do this. I just hope I don't throw up."

"If you do, try to do it somewhere discreet," he offered. "Maybe a big houseplant."

MARTINA ARRIVED at Cooper House on time, and she announced herself at the security intercom as instructed. The gate opened slowly, and she drove her Prius up the winding road to the house.

She'd seen pictures of Cooper House, of course. The place had been written up in the local paper several years ago when the previous owner had put it up for sale. Martina hadn't lived in Cambria then, but she'd searched for the article in the paper's computer archives after Alexis Sinclair's assistant had called.

Seeing the photos was one thing. Being here in the shadow of this looming mansion was an entirely different experience.

Three stories, a steep roofline broken up by gabled windows, a big wraparound porch, a widow's walk like a crown perched on the house's head. White gingerbread trim, and a turret with an onion dome roof.

The house was both magnificent and unsettling with its rich details and its brooding presence.

"Martina Russo?" A woman with her hair in a tidy bun was standing in the front doorway.

"Yes."

"Come in, please, and let's get started."

THE WOMAN, dressed in trim black slacks, a silk button-down shirt, and sensible low-heeled pumps, introduced herself as Margaret Nix, Ms. Sinclair's assistant. She offered Martina coffee or tea, both of which she declined.

They were sitting in the library, Ms. Nix behind a big oak desk and Martina in a fussy chair facing it.

"Ms. Sinclair asked me to get the preliminaries out of the way before she shows you the house. May I see your portfolio?" Ms. Nix stretched out a pale hand to receive it.

Martina handed it over. "Ah ... I have a list of clients who can serve as references, and my work was featured in *Central Coast Home* magaz—"

"We're aware." Ms. Nix cut Martina off in the middle of a word. She smiled with only her lips. "That's how you came to Ms. Sinclair's attention. If you don't mind, I'll just take a moment to review this."

"Of course."

Martina sat awkwardly, her hands in her lap, while the woman flipped through her portfolio. She wished she'd accepted a cup of tea so she'd have something to do with her hands while she waited.

After a few minutes, the woman gave Martina the non-smile again. "And your references?"

Martina pulled a file folder out of her bag and handed it over.

"Will I get to meet Ms. Sinclair or Mr. Mills soon? Because—"

Ms. Nix held up one finger to silence Martina without looking up from her reading.

Martina was beginning to wonder whether the woman would deem her qualifications unsatisfactory and usher her out the door. Instead, she closed the portfolio and the file folder, handed them back to Martina, and stood up.

"If you'll excuse me for just a moment."

She walked out of the room, leaving Martina alone.

Martina had never been able to resist inspecting an interesting space—let alone one where she'd been left unsupervised. She got up and walked slowly around the room, marveling at the built-in oak bookcases, the fireplace, and the antique rug that stretched nearly wall to wall over the gleaming wood floors. Having taken all of that in, she turned her attention to the books—volume after volume filling the floor-to-ceiling bookcases.

Was Mills a reader? Was Alexis Sinclair? Were these just for show, or did someone love them? Had they come with the house?

She had just pulled a leather-bound book off a shelf and was leafing through it when the door opened and another woman walked in—one she recognized from the internet as Alexis Sinclair.

"Oh, those dusty old things." She walked over to Martina and extended her hand stiffly, probably in a way intended to best show off her manicured nails. "Alexis Sinclair."

"Martina Russo. It's lovely to meet you, Ms. Sinclair."

"Oh, call me Alexis. I'm so glad you could come. I can't wait to hear your ideas for the house. It's just a wreck, isn't it?" She smiled expectantly, as though waiting for Martina to agree that the house was little better than a teardown.

If that was what Martina was expected to say, she couldn't do it. "Well, I'm sure there are ways it could use some updating, but ... what I've seen of the house is magnificent."

"Oh!" Alexis laughed as though Martina had made a particularly witty joke. "We'll see about that once you've had the tour."

~

MARTINA COULD HAVE BEEN honest and told Alexis that, as much as she wanted to tear the place down to the studs and start from scratch just for the experience, the house didn't need it. Now that she was here, she saw with some disappointment that there was very little she would change about Cooper House. True, she wouldn't mind playing with the overly modernized kitchen a bit to bring it more into harmony with its Victorian roots. But otherwise, she would barely touch a thing.

But this job could make her career. And if she'd learned one thing as an interior designer, it was how to tell rich people what they wanted to hear.

So, as the two of them went from room to room, assessing the state of Cooper House's aesthetics, Martina made all of the right noises to impress her hostess.

"The master bathroom is a bit small and dark, isn't it?" she observed as they made their way through the second floor.

"Oh, darling, yes. What would you suggest?"

Martina poked around in the bathroom, peeking into a closet, then going out into the hallway and looking into the next room. Then she returned to where Alexis was waiting for her.

"If you're not using the bedroom next door for anything essential, I'd suggest expanding the bathroom to create a true spa experience. Deep soaking tub, expansive walk-in shower with multiple shower-heads, a heated towel rack, radiant heating under the floor tiles. We could put in a big window here"—she indicated a space on the wall —"and add a large dressing room here."

"A dressing room?"

From the way Alexis's face had transformed, Martina knew she'd said the magic words.

"Oh, yes. We can put in shelving for your shoes, drawers for your lingerie, plenty of space for hanging clothing, a full-length three-way mirror with lighting, an upholstered bench in the center, and"— Martina scrambled to imagine what else a woman like this might want—"of course, a large vanity over here, where you can sit comfortably and do your hair and makeup." She motioned to where this mythical station of narcissism might be positioned.

"Wonderful." Alexis clasped her hands together between her breasts. "Chris just doesn't understand why I can't make do with the existing bathroom." She rolled her eyes. "Men have no idea."

In fact, Martina also had no idea why Alexis couldn't make do with what she had, but this was no time to tell her that. Martina wanted the job, and she knew what she had to say to get it.

She also knew this wasn't Alexis's house—it was Christopher Mills's place. Mills would be writing the checks for Martina's work, so Alexis wasn't the only person Martina would have to impress.

"What about Mr. Mills?" Martina asked as they moved on from the master suite to the in-home gym. "Will he be joining us?"

"Oh." Alexis waved a hand as though her boyfriend—the owner of the home they were talking about—were of no importance. "I'll have you pop in to say hello before you leave."

As though Martina's meeting with Mills would be merely a casual social hello rather than a make-or-break event in her career.

"I can't wait," she said.

3

Martina had a lot of things running through her head as Alexis led her to meet Christopher Mills, tech genius, the man who would decide whether her own career would suddenly be launched into the stratosphere.

For one thing, she wondered why the man was letting his girlfriend make all of the decisions about redesigning his house. Was Alexis more than a girlfriend? Surely they had to be serious if he was giving her this kind of influence.

For another thing, she wondered how much input he would want into the redesign process. He owned the place—he must have opinions on what it should look like and how it should function. If he didn't, that would raise more than one red flag. The last thing Martina wanted was to put months of work into the job—with the corresponding cost to her client—and then find out that he hated it.

Her other questions had more to do with her own curiosity than with any professional concern. Last she'd heard, he was living in Silicon Valley, but if he wanted a complete update of Cooper House, did that mean he was here to stay? What was he like? Would he resemble the tech moguls she saw on the news or in books? Was he socially awkward? Did he wear the same clothes every day?

All of this was playing through her mind as Alexis ushered her down a long hallway on the second floor and into a large room dominated by built-in glass cases containing a multitude of small, colorful items.

At first, it didn't register what those small, colorful items were.

"Martina, I'd like you to meet Christopher." Alexis led Martina to a man who was standing near one of the glass cases, holding one of the small objects. "You'll have to excuse him; he's playing with his toys."

"His ... excuse me?" Martina took a closer look and saw that the objects were superhero action figures—hundreds, maybe thousands of them. The man in front of her was holding what Martina recognized from the movies as Ant-Man. Now that she thought of it, she might have remembered reading something about the action-figure room. She extended her hand. "Mr. Mills, I'm pleased to meet you."

"Call me Chris." He shook her hand and put the little figure back into its spot in the case between Spider-Man and the Human Torch.

"I'll just leave you two to get to know each other," Alexis said. "I have to find Margaret to discuss my schedule. I've been so busy." She rolled her eyes to indicate the sheer magnitude of her overtaxed state. "Martina, we'll talk soon."

Then she was gone, and Martina was left alone with Chris. She assessed him as he rearranged a couple of his action figures, closed the glass door, then turned to her.

At around five-foot-eight, he was only slightly taller than Martina. He was young—probably no older than thirty-five or thirty-six—with medium brown hair cut short, blue eyes, a slim, athletic build, and a smile that said something about you amused him, though you might be better off not knowing what it was.

He gestured toward a pair of club chairs separated by a small table. "Please, have a seat." Once they both were settled in, he asked, "So, how did things go with Alexis?"

"Very well." Martina nodded enthusiastically, as though she and Alexis had bonded like sisters. In fact, Martina had taken an immediate dislike to the woman, but it wouldn't be the first time she'd

failed to connect personally with a client. There was no reason it had
to interfere with the job.

They chatted a bit about Cooper House, its history, and—
answering one of Martina's questions—Chris's plan to stay there
indefinitely.

"So, how soon can you start?" he asked.

Martina's mouth fell open. She realized how she must look and
hurried to compose her features. "I ... ah ... I can start right away. But,
don't you want to check my references? Review my portfolio? Discuss
my ideas for the—"

He waved her off. "Whatever Alexis wants is fine. Except"—he
shifted a bit in his seat, as though the topic made him uncomfortable
—"don't change this room. It's off-limits."

Martina looked around. Aside from the glass cases of action
figures and the chairs in which Chris and Martina were sitting, the
room contained a sofa—older and more worn than the other furniture in the house—a big-screen TV, a wet bar with refrigerator, and a
large oak desk covered in computer equipment.

There wasn't a hint of Alexis in this room, and, apparently, he
wanted to keep it that way.

"Of course." Martina tried to keep her curiosity in check. She'd
gotten the job, so the less she said at this point, the better. Still, she
couldn't seem to help herself, so she phrased things as delicately and
tactfully as she could. "So, you must really trust Alexis's judgment on
this. How long have you two been together?" Martina peeked at his
left ring finger and found it bare.

"Oh ... a few months."

A few *months*? And he was handing over the redesign of his house
to her? She tried not to show her surprise—or her dismay. "I see. And
... what does Alexis do professionally?" The woman had a full-time
assistant and had talked about being intolerably busy—was she a
CEO? A corporate lawyer? Was she someone high-placed in the
entertainment industry?"

"Alexis doesn't work," he said.

Martina was getting a lot of practice controlling her facial expressions—a skill that was proving to be essential in this conversation. "Oh. It's just, she has Margaret, and she talked about being very busy. ..."

"She's very busy being Alexis."

Was that twitch of his mouth a smirk? Martina was sure it was.

"And," he continued, "being in a relationship with me is apparently an exhausting full-time job. So. What's the first step in getting this project underway?"

MARTINA, like Alexis, had a full schedule. She checked on a job she had in progress in Cambria's Park Hill neighborhood; she called the general contractor she worked with to talk about his schedule; and she went home and worked on the CAD program on her computer for a while, putting together a proposal for a kitchen redesign in Pine Knolls. Then she checked out the real estate websites, something she regularly did to scope out what was being bought and sold. She had relationships with several Realtors in Cambria who passed her name along to clients who either had to get a house in shape to sell or who were buying a fixer-upper that needed some professional loving care.

Any spin through the real estate sites inevitably led to Martina fantasizing about her own house—the one she would buy one day, hopefully sooner than later, to transform into her dream home. A home where she would live with her eventual husband and children. She was just scanning the photos of a three-bedroom on Lodge Hill when Benny came home.

At last, Martina could talk to someone about her odd encounter with Christopher Mills—something she'd been dying to do since the moment she'd left Cooper House.

"Hey." Benny tossed her bag onto the floor next to the sofa and went to the refrigerator for a bottle of iced tea. She came back into the living room with the tea, twisted off the cap, and took a drink. "How'd the Cooper House thing go?"

"I got the job," Martina said.

"You did?" Benny let out a celebratory whoop. "Holy shit! Congratulations, that's amazing!"

"It is," Martina agreed. "It really is. But …"

"But what?"

"But it's weird." Martina filled her sister in on the details of the weirdness—how Alexis didn't work but had a full-time assistant; how Mills didn't seem to care what Martina did with his house; how Chris and Alexis had only been together for a few months, but he was letting Alexis spend what would certainly be hundreds of thousands of dollars on Cooper House. "I mean, that's strange, right? Usually at this stage in a relationship, you're considering whether to give someone a drawer."

"And he's turned over his whole house," Benny finished for her.

"Well, not his whole house. He's not letting me touch his action-figure room." Martina told her sister about the room, with its display of toys and its shabby, lived-in feeling in contrast to the fine polish of the rest of the house.

Benny was perched on the arm of the sofa, her feet, now bare, resting on the cushions. She pointed one finger at Martina. "That's the real him, I'll bet my own ass—the action figures and the messy desk and the tacky sofa. The rest of the place is how he thinks a rich guy ought to live. But that one room, the one he won't let you touch? That's where he lets down his guard and lets himself just … be."

"And Alexis made fun of it," Martina observed.

"Uh-oh."

"Just a little. When she brought me into the room, she told me about his 'toys,' and her tone was sort of … mocking."

"Yikes."

"Yeah." They both considered the implications of that.

Finally, Benny said, "If that room is so important to him, so personal, that he won't let you change it, and his new girlfriend thinks it's stupid …"

"I'll be lucky if I get halfway through the project before they break up," Martina concluded. She'd be redesigning a house to the specifications of someone who would no longer be living in it.

She was wondering if she'd be crazy to take the job. On the other hand, she'd almost certainly be crazier not to—so, of course, she would take it. She was about to embark on the biggest job of her career so far, possibly the biggest job she would ever have.

Regardless of her clients' relationship status, that called for a celebration.

Martina called Bianca and Sofia, who stopped by a wine shop on their way home from work and bought a cold bottle of champagne. When they got to the house, Martina poured the wine for herself, Sofia, and Benny, and a Perrier for Bianca. Then they all stood in the kitchen and toasted Martina's good fortune.

"To Martina. May this job lead you to become a hot celebrity designer with your own HGTV show," Benny said, and they all clinked glasses.

"From your lips to God's ears," Martina said, and drank.

Privately, she thought she could do without the HGTV show. She'd be happy if she just got to finish the work before the Chris Mills–Alexis Sinclair relationship blew up—and if she, herself, were far away from the destruction when it happened.

4

The first step in the Cooper House job was to create a preliminary plan and draw up a proposal to present to Chris and Alexis. For that, Martina needed her contractor.

She consulted with Alexis's assistant and with Noah Barrett, the general contractor she usually worked with, and arranged for herself and Noah to visit Cooper House.

They arrived on a Friday at two p.m. A crisp November chill was in the air, and fog from the ocean covered the landscape in its soft, gray blanket.

"This place looks like it should be in some Gothic novel about a ghost kid and her crazy uncle who lives in the attic," Noah said as they crunched their way across the gravel leading toward the house.

"I know, right?" Martina grinned. "I love it. I don't think it needs as many changes as Alexis wants, but ... still. I can't wait to get my hands on it."

She'd expected Noah to be as giddy as she was over the idea of working on Cooper House. But she should have realized Noah didn't get giddy. He was a highly practical man who'd been working in the Cambria area for decades, had built and repaired the houses of the rich, and was impressed by very little.

"I just hope this guy and his girlfriend aren't assholes," Noah remarked as they headed up the front porch steps.

TWENTY MINUTES LATER, neither of them had much reassurance about the asshole factor. Chris and Alexis had both failed to show their faces, and Martina and Noah were working with Margaret instead.

The woman was efficient and businesslike, which was a plus, but Martina had expected the couple to take more interest in how their house was going to look.

"Excuse me, Margaret. Will Chris or Alexis be joining us?" Martina asked when she'd held in the question as long as she could.

Margaret looked surprised, her carefully lipsticked mouth forming an O. "No. I'm sorry. I thought you understood you'd be consulting with me today."

"Oh. It's just ... I'll be making preliminary plans for the first phase of the remodel, and I might have questions that—"

"I'm here to answer your questions." Margaret, who appeared to be in her mid twenties and who surely should have been doing something more fun with her life, smiled winningly. "Alexis has discussed her priorities with me, and she has given me her full authorization to go forward."

Martina could tell by the look on the woman's face that few things gave her as much pride as having Alexis's full authorization.

"All right." Martina rallied. "Let's focus on the rooms I know she cares most about based on our conversation last week."

NOAH KEPT his face neutral and his thoughts to himself until he and Martina were in the spare bedroom that would be turned into Alexis's dressing room. Margaret had gotten a text on her cell phone and had excused herself to go God knew where and do God knew what.

Once she was gone and they were left alone—ostensibly to assess which walls should be taken down or moved and what that would involve—Noah shot Martina a look she'd seen before, one that meant somebody was a real piece of work.

"You said Alexis doesn't have a job?" he asked.

"That's what Chris told me."

"And she's got an assistant at her beck and call."

"Apparently."

"What for?"

Martina peeked toward the door to make sure they were still alone, and said, "Chris says it's a full-time job just being Alexis."

"He said that?"

"Yes."

Noah's eyebrows shot upward, and he let out a long, slow whistle. "Trouble in paradise."

"I guess so."

They'd barely finished the exchange when they heard voices coming from the next room—the master bedroom. At first, the voices were just murmurs, indistinct and undecipherable. Then the volume began to rise, and the gist of the conversation came through.

"Well, if *that's* how you feel, Christopher, then I don't—"

"Don't. Don't make it about me. Don't pretend I'm the problem here."

"The *problem*? Is that how you see me, Christopher? As a *problem*?"

"For God's sake, I didn't say that. Alexis—"

More murmurs, then a couple of thumps. Then Chris's voice again: "What are you doing? Where do you think you're going?"

"Somewhere I'm *appreciated*! Somewhere where I can—" They didn't get the next few words, but they did get the final three: "So *fuck you!*"

Martina and Noah both flinched at the sound of something hitting the wall that separated the two rooms—something that had to have been made of glass or china, or maybe ceramics. Whatever it was, they heard it break into pieces.

"Oh, shit." Noah's face broke into something like awed delight, and he let out a low laugh. "Rich people, man."

Martina felt close to tears. She could feel the biggest job of her life slipping away before it had even started.

AFTER A DOOR HAD SLAMMED and they'd heard the sound of feminine feet stomping through the hallway and down the stairs, Noah and Martina looked at each other.

"Maybe we should take a break," Martina said.

"Sure. I'm gonna step outside and call my guys." Noah had subcontractors working on a couple of different jobs across town, and he regularly called in to check on their progress.

Once he was gone, Martina wondered what to do. She didn't want to keep working if the job was off, but she didn't want to leave yet, either.

She decided to head down to the main floor to look for Margaret —maybe she'd know what the hell was going on.

Martina gathered her things, walked into the hallway, and headed toward the main staircase. On her way, she passed the open door to the master bedroom.

She peeked inside—she couldn't help it—and there was Chris, standing with his back to her, looking out the window, his shoulders slumped and his posture saying he was a man in pain.

Oh, God. She couldn't just leave him like that, could she? She couldn't just walk away and pretend she hadn't heard what she'd heard or seen what she'd seen.

She knocked delicately on the open door. "Um ... Chris?"

He looked up as though coming out of a dream, then rubbed his eyes with his fingertips. "Ms. Russo."

"Martina."

"Martina. Right." He massaged the back of his neck with one hand, looking tired. "I guess you heard all of that. I'm sorry. That must have been awkward."

"Don't worry about that." She came into the room a few steps. "Are you okay?"

WHEN WAS the last time someone had asked Chris if he was okay, and then seemed to really care about the answer? He couldn't remember. It had been so long he barely recalled how one was supposed to respond.

You're supposed to say you're fine, even if you're not. You're supposed to lie.

"Yes, of course. I'm good. I'm ... everything's fine."

Martina looked to one side of the room, where Alexis had dented the wall when she'd hurled a crystal vase into it. Hundreds of shards were sprinkled on the floor, glinting in the light from a nearby lamp. "It doesn't look like everything's fine," she said.

"Well ..."

"Come downstairs to the kitchen. I'll make you a cup of herbal tea."

The idea of her making tea for him out of the goodness of her heart and not because she was being paid to do it appealed to him. Still, he felt self-conscious about having put her in this position.

"You don't have to do that. Besides, I don't think we have any herbal tea."

"Let me take care of that." She took his arm and guided him toward the hallway. "Come on."

MARTINA POKED around in the pantry while Chris sat on a barstool nearby. He was right—they didn't have any herbal tea. She was sure she'd seen an herb garden on her way in; that was even better.

She found a pair of kitchen scissors in a drawer, told him to sit tight, and went outside and down the front steps. To one side of the front walkway, she found some potted herbs. She snipped some mint, then went back inside. In the kitchen, she rinsed the mint leaves, then hunted around for a kettle and put some water on to boil.

"You're making mint tea," he observed.

"Yes."

"From scratch."

"Well ... yes." She made tea from herbs nearly every day at home; surely it wasn't some amazing feat.

"I didn't even know we had herbs out there." He sounded exhausted.

Martina put one fist on her cocked hip and gaped at him. "How is that possible? It's your house."

He shook his head and rubbed his forehead. "We have gardeners."

"Of course you do."

The kettle whistled, and Martina turned off the heat. She poured the water into a teapot where she'd placed the fresh mint leaves. Then she put the lid on the pot and waited for it to steep.

When it was done, she poured the tea into a cup, added a little of the honey she'd found in the pantry, and placed the steaming mug in front of him.

"You didn't know you had herbs, and you don't seem to care what I do with your house," Martina said. "Who's living your life, anyway? Because it doesn't seem to be you."

The second it was out of her mouth, she knew she'd stepped over a line—and she was desperate to get back to the other side of it. "Oh, God. I'm sorry. I shouldn't have said that. I'm an idiot."

He looked at her impassively. "That would make two of us, apparently."

"Please, I didn't—"

"Forget it." He took a sip of his tea. "This is really good."

"Oh. I'm glad." She pulled up a barstool next to his and sat down. "Are you sure you're okay?"

He looked into the tea, his mug in both hands. For a moment, it seemed like he might answer her honestly—like he might say something both true and real. Then a slight smile played on his lips. "Of course. I'm fine. Alexis will be back. She always comes back. She just needs some space."

"She's done this before?" Martina was aware she sounded horrified, and she made an effort to control her tone. "I mean, you two have been having problems for a while, then?"

Something changed then. That was the moment, apparently, when she'd pried too much, stuck her nose in too far. He put down his tea, stood up, and extended his hand for her to shake.

"Thank you for coming today, Martina. Let's call it a day, all right? I'll be in touch." He shook her hand, then led her toward the door. "I'll see you out."

Before she could protest, Martina had been deposited on the front porch, and the front door closed behind her.

She found Noah outside near his truck and told him he might as well go check on his other job sites.

"So that's it, then?" he said.

Martina, near tears, shrugged. "I don't know, Noah. We'll see."

5

Chris woke up alone the next morning after a night of too little sleep. He didn't know when Alexis would be back, but he thought she would return eventually, after she decided he'd suffered enough.

The fact that he was with someone who enjoyed making him suffer almost certainly bore some introspection. But not this morning. This morning, he just needed to have some coffee and clear his head.

He got out of bed, ran his hands through his hair, pulled on a pair of sweatpants, and headed downstairs to make coffee. If Alexis were here, someone would be making the coffee for him—she had people to do that kind of thing—but she wasn't, so he was on his own.

That was fine. He preferred to go through the details of his day without people breathing down his neck.

Downstairs in the kitchen, a cavernous room full of professional quality appliances, he hunted up some French roast and got the coffee going. He leaned his butt against the counter and rubbed at his face while he waited for it to brew.

When it was done, he found a mug and poured. The process made him think about hot drinks in general, which made him think about tea, which made him think about Martina Russo brewing mint tea for him from leaves she'd found in the garden.

He hadn't known a person could do that. To him, tea came in tidy little bags that you dunked into your mug by their square paper tags.

Intriguing.

He took a sip of his coffee and winced because it was strong and hot—exactly the way he needed it to be. He carried the mug outside, where he stood on his front porch, looked out over the landscape of rolling hills dotted with oaks and pines, and considered his options.

Alexis certainly wanted him to leave Cambria and come after her. He'd done this dance before, with Alexis and with women who had come before her: she wanted something, he failed to give it to her, she stormed off in a flurry of obscenities and broken glassware, and he chased after her, soothing her and ultimately giving her whatever she'd wanted in the first place.

He was starting to think it was time to break the cycle. If he didn't follow her—if he didn't play his part—what then? She'd come back, probably. This relationship meant too much to her social status for it to end that easily. Maybe when she returned, they could talk—really talk—about what they both could do to stop playing this game.

Chris didn't think it was all Alexis's fault. If it were, this would be an anomaly.

It wasn't.

He seemed to get involved in one problem relationship after another, and it was time to get off the roller coaster—stop the endless dysfunction. If he could make things work with Alexis, he'd do it without playing into her efforts to manipulate him.

It was best for him to stay the course, pretend nothing had happened, go about his life, and wait for her to come back.

And if part of him felt relieved that she'd left? Well. He could think about that another day.

~

THAT MORNING, a Saturday, all four of the Russo sisters gathered at the house to address invitations to Sofia's wedding. They had almost four months until the ceremony, so the invitations wouldn't be mailed yet, but Sofia wanted to have them done and ready to go. They'd sent out save-the-date cards months before, but the invitations would make things official.

The women sat around the big kitchen table with mimosas for Sofia, Martina, and Benny, and plain orange juice for Bianca. An occasion that involved wedding invitations seemed like it should also involve mimosas.

"Why isn't Patrick helping us? It's his wedding, too," Benny groused as she stuck a stamp on a response envelope.

"He offered." Sofia plucked a fresh invitation from the pile in the middle of the table. "His handwriting is illegible."

"I'm supposed to be the one with illegible handwriting," Bianca commented. "I'm the doctor."

Martina peered across the table to look at Bianca's writing. "Jeez. Yours is pretty good. Better than mine."

"Well, I'm making an extra effort for Sofia's sake." Bianca gave Sofia a sweet smile.

"Which I appreciate," Sofia said. "But can you hurry up? I don't want to be at this all day."

They worked for a while, discussing the bridesmaid dresses, the appetizer menu, and the reception venue.

"Speaking of fabulous venues, how did things go at Cooper House yesterday?" Bianca glanced up from what she was writing to look at Martina.

Martina groaned. "It was such an epic disaster that I'm trying not to think about it."

Everyone stopped working to focus on her.

"What happened? Why didn't you say anything?" Sofia asked.

Martina shrugged. "I don't know. I just … I wasn't ready to talk about it. I think the job's off." Damn it, she was starting to get misty-eyed. "I know I shouldn't get emotional—it's just a job. There'll be others. But this was a really big opportunity, and I just …" She shrugged again.

"Okay, back up," Benny said. "What happened?"

Martina told the whole story—how she and Noah had arrived to find Margaret waiting for them with Alexis and Chris nowhere in sight. How they'd begun assessing Martina's plan to turn a spare bedroom into a dressing room for Alexis. How they'd heard the fight in the next room, and how Alexis had stormed off. And finally, she told them about her conversation with Chris over mint tea.

"Oh, shit. You knew this was going to happen," Benny said. "You predicted things wouldn't last between those two."

"Yeah, but I thought I'd at least get more than an hour into the job before it all went to hell," Martina said miserably.

"So, that's it, then?" Sofia asked. "I mean, they're broken up?"

"Who knows?" Martina threw her hands into the air. "He says she'll be back. Like this happens all the time. Maybe it does! Who knows what kind of dysfunctional freak show of a relationship they've got going on?"

"So, what are you going to do?" Bianca asked.

"I'm going to wait until Monday, then call Margaret, Alexis's assistant. She seems to be pretty efficient. She'll know what I should do. In the meantime, somebody give me another mimosa."

Benny got up, took Martina's glass into the kitchen, and came back with a fresh mimosa. "Drink up. Sounds like you need it."

BY THE TIME Martina made the call to Margaret on Monday morning, she had more or less come to terms with the idea that the job was going to be canceled. No money had changed hands, and no contracts had yet been signed. Either side could have called things off based on something as simple as a hunch or a rumor, let alone the complete collapse of Chris and Alexis's relationship.

As she entered the number on her cell phone, she told herself to stay professional, leave emotion out of it. There would be other jobs. There would be other opportunities.

When Margaret picked up the phone, she sounded as crisp and efficient as ever. "Good morning, Martina. How may I help you?"

"Well, I ... I was just wondering ... I haven't heard from Chris or Alexis since Friday, and I thought ..." So much for being professional. She was babbling.

"Whatever it is, I'll see if I can help." Margaret's reply sounded so much better than what she probably wanted to say, which was, *Oh, for God's sake, spit it out already.*

Martina took a steadying breath and said what she'd called to say. "I'd like to know whether the Cooper House job is still happening. If not, I need to focus on my other clients." She closed her eyes and waited for the bad news.

"Why wouldn't it be happening?"

Whatever Martina had expected to hear, it wasn't that. "Well ... it's just ... on Friday, when I was at Cooper House, Chris and Alexis had a big fight, and ... Not that I'm trying to stick my nose in where it doesn't belong, but ... she left, and I ..." She was babbling again. Martina willed herself to stop it.

Margaret was silent for a moment. When she spoke, her voice was composed, professional—and the slightest bit sympathetic. "Martina, I'm not sure what you overheard on Friday or what you might have assumed. But Alexis merely went to the Bay Area for the weekend to visit friends. It was a trip she'd had planned for days."

"Really? But—"

"I'm so sorry things were cut short on Friday after I was called away. When can you come to the house and resume your work?"

Martina scowled, opened her mouth, then closed it again. "Are you sure?" Margaret was talking as though what happened hadn't happened at all.

"Of course. Let me get my book so we can reschedule. Now, what time works best for you?"

~

WHEN SHE GOT off the phone, Martina called Noah to consult.

"Apparently, we're in some kind of upside-down world where Chris and Alexis never had that fight, their relationship is one hundred percent solid, and the part where she broke things and threw the F-word around was just a product of our overactive imaginations," she told him.

"Interesting. What about the part where our livelihoods depend on the two of them keeping their shit together?" Noah asked.

"We didn't discuss that part."

"Ah."

"In any event," Martina went on, "Margaret wants to know when we'll be there. So, what do you think? Do we go ahead with it?"

Noah made a scoffing noise. "Of course we go ahead with it. It's Cooper House. The chance to work on that place is worth putting up with a considerable amount of bullshit."

"Right." That was pretty much what Martina had concluded, too. She just wondered how much bullshit, exactly, they were in for.

6

Martina made an appointment for herself and Noah to return to Cooper House that Wednesday morning to resume their work. Her plan was to follow Margaret's lead and pretend nothing untoward had happened.

Clearly something had happened, though, because Alexis still wasn't back. Margaret said Alexis had been "detained" in the Bay Area by "unforeseen circumstances." Martina and Noah exchanged looks when she said it, but they let it go without comment.

"This thing's a clusterfuck waiting to happen," Noah remarked as soon as Margaret left the room.

Martina couldn't say she disagreed.

BECAUSE THE HOUSE was so big and Alexis had expressed a desire to change a large part of it, Martina's plan was to separate the work into four phases, each with its own budget and timeline.

For now, she was focused on Phase One: the master suite and several other areas Alexis had indicated were high priority, including the kitchen, the library, the formal dining room, and the foyer.

"Oh, and Chris's study. The room with the action figures," Margaret said, looking over Martina's shoulder at her notes.

"What?" Martina looked at the woman in alarm. "Chris said that was off-limits."

"Did he?" Margaret's brow furrowed. "I wasn't aware. Alexis specifically instructed me to prioritize it." She lowered her voice slightly. "Have you seen it?" She shuddered. "The décor is mid-century college dorm."

"I've seen it."

"Then you know." Margaret jotted something down in her leather-bound agenda, then closed the book and adjusted her glasses. "Well, I'll leave you to it."

When she was gone, Noah let out a low laugh. "This ought to be good."

∼

MARTINA WAS in no hurry to talk to Chris about his study and whether it was, or was not, off-limits. Part of her was certain the ensuing conflict between Chris and Alexis would destroy her beautiful little fantasy in which she finished the Cooper House job, found fame and fortune, and lived happily ever after.

She worked on her plan for the rest of Phase One instead, reasoning that she could have that conversation with him later.

Martina and Noah took photos and measurements. She jotted sketches and notes into her notebook, and he gave his input on load-bearing and non-load-bearing walls, the necessity and practicality of moving electrical wires and plumbing, the possible complications that might come with such relocations, and the need for various permits and inspections.

By lunchtime, Martina thought she had enough information from Noah for him to go and attend to other projects he had in the works.

"What about you? You knocking off?" Noah asked.

"I'd better stay and talk to Chris. I can't avoid the question of the action-figure room forever." Just saying it caused a pit of dread to form in her stomach.

"You want me to stay around for moral support?"

"No, you go. I'll be fine. If this thing is going to blow sky high, it's better if it happens sooner rather than later."

"Good point." Noah smacked her companionably on the back. "Good luck, slugger. Let me know how it goes."

Martina found Chris sitting behind his desk in his study, tapping something into his computer keyboard. He looked more relaxed than he had when she'd seen him before, and somehow younger, too. He was wearing jeans and a gray T-shirt, his sock-clad feet up on the desk as he worked.

As Martina poked her head into the room, the action figures stared at her accusingly from their glass shelves.

She knocked softly on the open door. "Chris?"

He looked up as though he were emerging from underwater. Clearly, whatever he'd been working on had fully absorbed his attention. "Oh. Martina. Hi. Come on in." He sat up self-consciously, removing his feet from the desktop. "What can I do for you?"

She walked into the room, her messenger bag containing her phone, laptop, and notebook slung over her shoulder. "Ah ... there's something I have to ask you about."

He motioned to the chair across from his desk. "Sure. Have a seat."

She sat down, put the bag on the floor next to her chair, and folded her hands in her lap. She wasn't sure how to bring up the subject, so she just launched into it. "Margaret says I am to redesign this room during the first phase of the project. She said it's a high priority. I need to know how to proceed."

He blinked a couple of times. "She said that?"

"She did."

"Is that what Alexis told her?"

Martina didn't see any advantage to jumping into this particular dogfight. "You'll have to ask Margaret that."

He let out a harsh laugh. "Oh, I will. You bet your ass I will. But, Martina? The room stays the way it is."

~

CHRIS HAD BEEN TRYING to put the whole Alexis mess aside. She'd had one of her outbursts and had left him, for the moment. Fine. She was still instructing Margaret to move forward with the work on Cooper House, proving she intended to come back.

He was handling it. He was calmly waiting her out, which he was certain was the best approach. He wasn't going to chase her, but he'd be here when she decided to return. The whole thing was manageable.

But, by God, when had his house stopped being his house? When had he lost any claim to even the most private spaces in his own home?

And, perhaps a more important question: how many more pieces of himself was he willing to give up just to have a woman in his life?

None of that even touched on the way the dysfunction of his relationship had been put on full display in front of Martina. Part of him thought he shouldn't care about that, but what he *shouldn't* care about had very little bearing on what he *did* care about.

From the moment he'd met her, he'd cared very much about what Martina thought. Simple male vanity, probably, but there it was.

And now here she was, sitting in a chair across from his desk, looking at him with concern and sympathy. He didn't want her looking at him with concern or with sympathy. He wanted her looking at him with an entirely different set of feelings—but that didn't bear thinking about, not when he was already in a relationship.

Not that he'd be in one for much longer.

The expression on his face while he seethed about Alexis must have been unsettling, because Martina was scrambling to get up from her chair, gather her things, and get the hell out of there as quickly as possible.

"I'd better ... I'll just go." She hefted her bag and headed for the door.

He had to say something—anything so she wouldn't go home with an image of him as an enraged, egomaniacal asshole.

He went for an apology—he couldn't go too far wrong with that.

"I'm sorry about the confusion." He ran a hand through his hair. "We'll get things worked out, and I'll be in touch."

"All right." She paused with her hand on the doorknob and looked back at him. "May I ask you something?"

"Sure."

"You and Alexis don't seem to be ..." She hesitated. "You're not on the same page regarding the remodel. So, why are you doing it? It's your house. It should be the way you want it."

He considered answering her honestly—telling her he was doing it to pacify a woman who required constant pacifying. That spending tens or even hundreds of thousands of dollars changing a house that didn't need changing had seemed preferable to being alone.

But he wasn't quite ready to acknowledge the absurdity of his situation—namely, the fact that a man who'd made a fortune inventing a dating app couldn't find a healthy relationship to save his life.

"I'll call you," he said instead, and gave her a thin smile.

WHEN MARTINA WAS GONE, Chris's first instinct was to get in his car, drive to San Jose, storm into the condo he and Alexis shared, and tell her they were finished.

He couldn't keep doing this—couldn't keep working so hard to make her happy when he knew she'd never be happy. At least, not with him.

But he'd already resolved not to chase her, so he wouldn't.

He sat down at his desk, picked up the landline—his cell phone didn't get reliable service here—and called her.

Margaret, who was here in the house somewhere, answered.

"Margaret? I was calling Alexis," Chris said.

"She's had all of her calls forwarded to me." She said it as though that were a perfectly reasonable thing to be telling him.

"I need to speak to Alexis."

She hesitated. "Oh. This is awkward."

"What is?" He was beginning to get angry, but he didn't want to take it out on Margaret, who was just doing her job.

"Well ... Alexis very specifically told me not to put your calls through."

He let out a laugh at the pure gall of the woman. Of both of them, really.

"Margaret, I pay your salary."

"Yes, but I report to Alexis, so ... As I said, this is awkward."

He leaned back in his chair and rubbed his eyes with his free hand. "Margaret, since you're Alexis's assistant, I suggest that you ... go wherever she is. As soon as possible."

"But she specifically instructed me—"

"And now I'm specifically instructing you to get out of my house."

"But—"

"And when you see her," he said, trying to keep his voice neutral, "tell her it's over between us. She's welcome to contact me about getting her things from Cooper House. I'll expect her to move out of the condo, though she can take her time with that, as I don't plan to return anytime soon. Will you relay all of that, please?"

He hung up the phone feeling lighter than he had in a long time.

7

W ith the Cooper House job in limbo, Martina decided to focus on other things. She'd called Noah to tell him they were on hold until they heard from Chris. Now, there was nothing to do but turn her attention toward her other clients, Sofia's wedding, and her dream of buying a home of her own.

When Sofia had handed out wedding tasks nearly a year ago, Martina had been assigned to handle the bachelorette party, which was to be held the night before the wedding. That would be March 20, a Friday. Easy enough; they'd be gathering at a local bar, which didn't require much planning.

She was feeling smug about that when Bianca called her one evening after work to try to unload her own assignment.

"Please?" Bianca's voice held a whining tone that was rare for her. She usually was the most together, the most stoic, of the four of them. "Can you take the bridal shower? I'll owe you. I'll name my baby after you."

"Your baby's a boy."

"Please! I'll never ask you for anything again."

She'd heard that one before. All of the sisters regularly promised to never ask each other for anything again—and yet, here they were.

"But why? Isn't it all planned? At the last wedding prep meeting, you said it was under control."

Bianca was silent.

"It is under control, isn't it?" Martina asked.

"Well ..."

"Bianca!"

"Look. I didn't know it was going to be so hard to manage a pediatric practice while being pregnant. I thought ... you know, I'd just go about my life while being pregnant. How hard could that be? But I spent the first trimester hurling, and then the second trimester was all about getting caught up on the stuff I let slide during the first trimester."

"But—"

"And now," Bianca went on as though Martina hadn't spoken, "I've got to get the nursery ready, and buy a car seat and a crib, and oh, God, I'm so tired, Martina, so tired, because I'm already the size of a cement truck and I can't find a comfortable sleeping position."

"So, what you're saying is that it's not under control," Martina said dryly.

"And I'm supposed to be maid of honor!" Bianca said. "Which means I've got to write a speech, and the baby's going to be due about five minutes after the wedding, which means I'll be huge and my dress probably won't fit, and my water will probably break during the reception. I don't want to let Sofia down, but ... it's just a lot."

Martina's tone softened. "Oh, Bianca. Why didn't you say something before? We'd have pitched in. We'd have—"

"I'm saying something now. I need you to pitch in."

Martina was sitting on the edge of her bed, getting ready to change out of her work clothes and into a pair of yoga pants and a T-shirt. She sighed and slipped off her shoes. "Of course I'll do it. I'll take care of everything. Don't worry about a thing."

"Thank you, Martina. You know you're my favorite sister."

"Last week, Sofia was your favorite sister." Martina propped her foot up on the edge of the bed and massaged her toes; she'd been standing in heels much of the day, and her feet ached.

"Then it's really good you've got an edge on her now." Bianca already sounded perkier. "Seriously, thank you."

"No problem. Just let me know what you've got done on it so far."

Silence.

"I see," Martina said.

"Favorite sister," Bianca reminded her.

WHEN SHE'D FINISHED the phone call and was dressed in her comfortable home-for-the-night clothes, Martina made herself a cup of herbal tea and got settled at the kitchen table with her laptop to check the real estate listings.

Martina had been in the habit of checking the real estate websites since long before she'd decided to get her own place. It was relevant to her career as an interior designer, and anyway, she just loved houses—their spaces, their stories, their vast, unknowable potential.

The Cambria listings were usually a mixed bag of beachside behemoths, midrange single-family homes, and eccentric cabins.

When she called up the new listing in the Lodge Hill neighborhood, at first she wasn't sure what she was seeing. Initially, she thought it was a vacant lot because the main photo was of a grassy space dotted with towering pines, with no structure in sight.

On closer inspection, she saw there was a house—if you could call it that. Amid a gallery of twenty photos of the land—a glorious, riotous mix of wildflowers, trees, and native plants too numerous to list—was one photo of the house itself. Mid-century modern in style, the building was an oddly shaped structure with sharp angles and lots of glass, some of it broken. The front deck looked as though it had collapsed in places.

Martina squinted at the photo, suddenly recognizing the house.

She scrolled down to read the Realtor's text and gasped in shock and dismay.

All it takes is a little imagination!

A gorgeous half acre with water permit, available to build on immedi-

ately. Structure is a teardown, but this spectacular piece of land is the perfect place to put the house of your dreams! Call listing agent Riley Whittaker for details.

"Oh, my God!" Martina put her hand over her mouth, staring at her computer screen.

"What?" Benny, who'd gotten home ten minutes earlier, was walking past on her way to the refrigerator. "Did Gwyneth Paltrow say we're supposed to put something weird in our vaginas again?"

"Look at this." Martina spun her laptop around on the table so Benny could see it.

Benny bent to look at the screen, peering at the photo displayed there.

"It's a house," she said.

"Yes."

"A crappy house," Benny went on.

"It's the Hall house!" Martina exclaimed with some indignation. How could her sister not recognize it? Of course, Benny tended not to notice anything that didn't have gills and fins.

Benny looked at the picture and made a face. "If you'd said 'hell house,' that would have made more sense."

"Maxwell Hall!" Martina raised her voice as though an increase in volume would help Benny to know what she was talking about. "He was one of the most noted architects of the mid twentieth century! He built that house and lived in it for twenty years, from 1952 to 1972. And now they're advertising it as a teardown!"

The pure idiocy of that had Martina sputtering with indignation. Why would anyone want to destroy a Maxwell Hall house? And that didn't even touch on the fact that the house had been built to minimize its interference with the natural world around it, to blend in with its surroundings. What was likely to go in its place? A five-bedroom monstrosity with a three-car garage and a hot tub?

What about the oaks and pines that coexisted peacefully with the existing house? Would they be cut down to make way for some rich person's weekend getaway? What about the squirrels and deer and wild turkeys that roamed the parcel, grazing and foraging peacefully? What about the wildflowers that dotted the landscape?

Benny shrugged and continued on her way to find something to eat for dinner. "Maybe it won't even sell," she said.

Martina didn't respond, but she knew her sister was wrong. It would sell. Cambria had been in the grips of a severe drought until the rains of the past few years had ended it. As a result, the county wasn't allowing any new residential water service and hadn't for decades. If someone wanted to build a new house in Cambria, they either had to tear another one down or buy someone else's water permit at a cost of $200,000 or more.

A reasonably low-cost teardown—especially one on a good-sized lot—would be snapped up in no time.

"I have to do something about this," Martina said.

"Do something about what?" Sofia had come in the front door just in time to hear the last sentence of the conversation. She hung her purse on a hook just inside the door and came into the kitchen.

"The Maxwell Hall house on Lodge Hill is up for sale. They're advertising it as a teardown. Which is just ... just ..." She searched for a word. "Just criminal!"

Sofia looked at Martina and then at Benny. "Am I supposed to know who Maxwell Hall is? Because it's been a long day, and I'm so tired I'm not even sure who you two are."

She opened the refrigerator, took out a half-full bottle of chardonnay, and poured herself a glass. Then she turned to Martina, her hip leaning against the kitchen counter. "Wait. Is this that place off Pierce that's been falling apart for decades?"

"Yes!" Martina was gratified that at least Sofia had some idea what she was talking about.

Sofia grimaced at the memory of the place, much as Benny had when she'd looked at the photo. "I'd think tearing that place down would be a good thing. It's a safety hazard. I don't even think it's habitable."

"It's not. But that's not the point."

"Then what is?" Benny asked.

Martina snapped her laptop closed. "The point is, I'm going to save that house."

She just didn't know how she would do it, or if anyone besides her would care when she did.

———

8

C hris had expected fireworks when he sent the message through Margaret that he and Alexis were through. He'd expected yelling, fighting. He'd expected her to throw around obscenities, possibly some that questioned his parentage.

What he hadn't expected was to hear nothing at all.

Margaret had left the day he'd told her to go. A few days later, she'd contacted him to inquire about boxing and shipping Alexis's things to her new address in San Francisco.

Her new address. She wasn't at the condo anymore, and the address Margaret gave him wasn't her parents' place, either. Had she already found a place of her own, in this real estate market?

Curious, and more than a little bit suspicious, he had Googled the address and learned it belonged to a mutual acquaintance—a male acquaintance—whom Chris and Alexis had met at a charity ball a couple of months earlier.

The woman worked fast.

Or maybe she didn't—maybe she'd had it in the works for a while. Maybe she'd already been seeing the guy, and that was why she hadn't wanted to leave San Jose.

The man's net worth wasn't as high as Chris's, but it had to be pretty damned high. There was no way Alexis would be with him otherwise.

He knew it without a doubt—knew Alexis was only in it for the lifestyle—and that made him feel like an ass. Why had he wasted his time with someone who only saw him as a meal ticket? And why had he done the same thing with other women over and over again?

It was worth thinking about—probably in a therapist's office. But for now, he needed to take some time to adjust to his new reality.

LIVING in his cavernous house with only himself and his thoughts proved to be more than he could handle.

Since he'd sold his company, he didn't have anything to fill his time. And his own thoughts weren't nearly interesting enough to prevent him from succumbing to a deep, gnawing loneliness.

He was wandering around the place one morning, alone, thinking about his next move and whether he should return to his condo, when Martina Russo called him.

"I'm sorry to bother you," she said. It was midmorning, with bright light filtering through the windows of the library. He hadn't gotten dressed yet—he was barefoot, wearing only a pair of pajama pants.

"No bother. What's up?" He rubbed at the stubble on his chin— he hadn't bothered to shave lately—then tucked his free hand into his armpit as though he might be able to keep it safe there.

"It's just ... I wondered where we stood on the remodel. You said you'd be in touch, but I haven't heard back, and I have to work on my schedule for the coming month, so ..."

Shit. The remodel. In the turmoil of his current life, he'd forgotten about it.

"Ah. Of course. I'm sorry I haven't called." On top of everything else, he'd inconvenienced Martina, who'd only been doing her job. He'd need to get an invoice from her, pay for her time so far, apologize profusely ...

"That's perfectly fine," she said. "But I do need to know whether you're planning to go forward."

It was on the tip of his tongue to say no. To ask her what he owed her, then add a hefty bonus to compensate her for her trouble. But was that really what he wanted to do? He hadn't changed Cooper House much since he'd bought it. He'd never made it his own. Wasn't it time to do that? And anyway, the silence around here was about to drive him mad. A remodel would mean people, noise, activity.

And maybe even Martina making him cups of herbal tea.

"Of course we're going forward," he said. "When can you come over to get back to work? And ... bring your contractor. We're going to have to start from scratch."

THE MOOD at Cooper House was considerably different when Martina and Noah returned a couple of days later. For one thing, it was quieter, because Chris and Alexis weren't yelling at each other and throwing things.

Alexis wasn't there at all, in fact. Neither was Margaret, her hyper-efficient assistant.

"So, will we be working with Margaret today?" Martina asked when they first arrived.

"No, just me." Chris smiled, his hands stuffed into the pockets of his jeans.

"Oh. Really." Martina hadn't expected that answer, and it had thrown her off.

"Sure. Is that a problem?"

"Of course not. It's just ... you didn't seem all that interested in the details before."

"Things have changed," he said mildly. "Shall we get started?"

Chris walked her and Noah through the main rooms of the house, asking questions and making comments while Martina took notes.

"This kitchen looks like it belongs in a restaurant," he told her as they looked over the stainless steel countertops, the professional-quality appliances, the gigantic refrigerator. "I'd prefer one that looks like it belongs in a house."

Martina assessed the room with a critical eye. "Well, the size and the functionality certainly would come in handy if you were holding a big event. A catered dinner, maybe, or—"

"I don't plan to hold any big events."

No, clearly he didn't. She'd be surprised if he ever had anyone here at all, other than girlfriends. She walked around the room, looking at the shape of the space, the structure.

"I'm thinking this room was originally half the size," she said. "A smaller kitchen would have been more common in an original Victorian. A previous owner probably expanded it into a neighboring room, probably for a professional kitchen staff."

Noah pointed out a beam in the ceiling and said it likely had been the dividing point between rooms.

"What would it have looked like originally?" Chris asked. "In a typical house of this type, I mean."

"Here. I'll show you." Martina set her messenger bag on the counter, got out her laptop, and opened it. She did a search, clicked on a photo, and turned the laptop so he could see the screen. "See? The room would typically be fairly good size, but nothing like this one. A lot of the elements weren't very practical—you'd want modern appliances, obviously—but there are ways to make the room feel authentic while preserving functionality."

"Okay. Like what?" He leaned against the counter, his legs crossed at the ankles, watching her with interest.

"Well, we could take out this cabinetry here and add an antique farmhouse table." She motioned toward the area where the table would be. "We can install a farmhouse sink here, and some open shelving here. If this were an authentic Victorian kitchen, the flooring would probably be linoleum. Of course, you don't want that. I'd suggest a natural stone tile for durability as well as a period look."

She went on, telling him about the wonders of crown moldings, cabinetry with rich wood finishes, appliances hidden behind wood panels, and options for countertops—she suggested a mix of butcher block, matte zinc, and stone to mimic the look of mix-and-match furniture.

Now and then, she asked Noah questions about what was practical from a construction standpoint, and he grunted his answers.

"Do you cook much?" she asked Chris.

"Not much." He shrugged. "But coming into this room has always made me feel like I was sneaking into a hotel kitchen. Like the chef was going to chase me out any minute." He looked around thoughtfully. "I like your ideas. Let's start here. We'll do the kitchen, then we'll see about what comes next."

BY THE TIME Martina had taken photographs and measurements and had consulted with Noah on the practicalities of plumbing placement, lighting fixtures, and the possible moving of walls, she was feeling excited and energized. The idea of restoring this place—or, at least, one room of it—to something resembling its original spirit was more than she'd hoped for, especially after the blowup between Chris and Alexis. She couldn't wait to dive in.

Noah left by late morning. He had to get to another job site, and Martina had gotten the information from him that she needed. Now she had to draw up an initial schematic design with her ideas about the layout, finishes, and furniture for Chris's approval.

She was sitting at the kitchen counter happily taking notes when Chris, who had retreated from the room more than an hour ago to let her work, poked his head in the doorway.

"How's it coming along?" he asked.

"It's great. I'm just about done for today. I can't wait to have my way with your kitchen."

He gave her a mischievous grin and said, "Is that right?" in a way that made the whole thing sound dirty. She wasn't entirely sure she objected.

"Let me just finish my notes and I'll be out of your hair," she said.

"Okay, sure. No rush." He lingered in the doorway for a moment, watching her. "Or ..."

"Or?"

"Or, I could buy you lunch. As a way of apologizing for the rough start I put you through here."

Lunch? He wanted to buy her lunch? That was unexpected. There was something vulnerable in his face as he waited for her answer, something that told her he needed her to say yes. Alexis was clearly gone, and he was lonely after the breakup, that was all. He needed to talk to someone.

"All right."

His face brightened in a way she found heartbreaking. "Really? Great. Should we take my car?"

9

Martina had thought his car would be something showy —a Tesla, maybe, or a red Ferrari. She hadn't expected a car that was considerably older than she was, and certainly not one that growled uncomfortably when it ran, as though it were begging for mercy.

"This is your car?" As they stood inside one of the two three-car garages at Cooper House, she gaped at the oxidized aqua blue paint job, the primer, the small dent in the hood of Chris's 1965 Mustang.

"One of them, yeah." He beamed with pride as he looked at it. "I keep it here in Cambria for when I'm visiting, but Alexis wouldn't ride in it, so I had to sneak in time with it whenever I could. I guess that's not an issue anymore." He opened the passenger side door for her—it made a grinding screech—and she got in.

How to phrase the question delicately? "Have you ... had trouble finding someone to restore it?"

"I'm going to do it myself." He closed her door, came around to the driver's side, and got in beside her. His seat had been repaired with silver duct tape.

"Do you know how?" she asked. "To restore an old car, I mean?"

"No. That's why it's taking so long."

The car started with a roar, and they headed toward town.

IF CHRIS'S choice of car had surprised Martina, his restaurant selection did, as well. She'd thought he would want to go to Neptune or possibly The Sandpiper, or some other fine dining restaurant where he could eat in luxury and order the most expensive wine on the menu.

Instead, they went down Highway 1 to Duckie's Chowder House in Cayucos, a place next to the pier where you could order fish and chips and a Coke and have them at a counter facing the sidewalk as tourists in bathing suits and flip-flops walked by.

"You like fish and chips?" he asked as they stood in line waiting to order.

"I'm a vegetarian."

He nodded. "I should have known."

"What's that supposed to mean?"

"It just means ... look at you."

She looked down at herself: peasant skirt, Birkenstock sandals, white top—linen trimmed in lace. Her usual stack of bracelets, and rings on two of her toes.

She had to admit, he had a point.

He ordered the fish and chips, a cup of chowder, and a beer, and she had a garden salad with a side of garlic bread. They sat at a tall booth underneath a surfboard that had been mounted to the wall and waited for their food.

Initially, Martina wasn't sure what this was. Business? Social? Once he started asking questions about her interior design business, she relaxed a little. Clearly, it was business.

He asked about how she'd gotten her start in interior design, and she told him she'd always had an interest, starting from the time she'd made curtains and throw pillows for her Barbie DreamHouse. She'd gotten a bachelor's degree in interior architecture at the Rhode

Island School of Design, then had gone to work for a firm in Los Angeles after she graduated.

While she was talking, the waitress arrived bearing plates full of salad greens and fried fish. Chris poured some ketchup onto his plate, dunked a french fry, and bit off the end. "So, how did you end up in Cambria?" he asked.

She felt a knot in her gut, the way she always did when the subject came up. She tried to keep her face and her voice pleasant and neutral.

"I grew up here. And after I left, my parents still lived here. When they died a few years ago, my sisters and I inherited their house. It's a historic log cabin that used to be a brothel. We talked about selling it, or one of us buying out the others, but ... I don't think any of us could bear to give it up, because the house meant a lot to my mom and dad. They renovated it themselves." And, damn it, there she went—she could feel tears pooling in her eyes. She wiped them away with the tip of her napkin and forced out a laugh. "I'm sorry. It's an emotional topic."

"I didn't realize—"

"How could you? It's fine." She smiled to reinforce it. "And I'm fine, really. It just hits me sometimes."

She worried he might ask the next natural question: *How did they die?* Instead, mercifully, he changed the subject slightly.

"So, you live there with your sisters?"

"Two of them. Benny—that's short for Benedetta—and Sofia. And Sofia's fiancé. My other sister, Bianca, used to live there, too, but she moved out after she got married. She and her husband have a place across town."

All of this talk about her, her family, and her personal life was unsettling. Martina took a big bite of salad so she'd have an excuse not to go on about it. Then, when she'd had a moment to regroup, she shifted the conversation back to Cooper House and the redesign.

"So, how did you find me? I mean, you can afford anyone you want. I would have thought you'd call some celebrity designer up in the Bay Area and bring them down for the job."

He nodded. "That's what Alexis wanted to do."

"So, why didn't you?" She took a sip of her iced tea.

He shrugged. "Your name was on the front of *Central Coast Home* magazine, and that issue just happened to be lying around when Alexis and I started talking about a remodel."

"That's it?"

"That's it."

"You didn't ask around? You didn't ... I don't know ... get competitive bids?"

"Well, I suppose we would have, but Alexis liked your ideas about the master bedroom dressing room thing, so ..." He shrugged again.

"You let Alexis decide."

"Sure. Why not?"

So much of this just wasn't adding up. It seemed off. Should she ask the question that was on her mind? That might put him off, and it might be unprofessional. Still ...

"Can I ask you something?" she said.

"Shoot."

"You were going to let Alexis have your house redone. You were going to let her—or, really, her and Margaret—decide the whole thing."

"That's not a question."

She poked at her salad, then continued. "It's just ... your style is completely different than hers. And you don't want the same things for the house that she does. And you two seemed to be on shaky ground...."

"That's still not a question."

She looked up from her plate and focused on him. "Why were you going to let her do it? Why were you going to let her change your house in ways you didn't want, when I'm guessing you knew the relationship was almost over anyway?"

He hesitated only a moment, then said, "You're right. I knew it was almost over. I was trying to make her happy, that's all. But I couldn't. It didn't work."

SHIT. He hadn't meant to tell her that. He hadn't meant to lay out all of his vulnerability—and, let's face it, his idiocy—to someone he'd just met. But he hadn't talked to anyone in an open, honest way in a long time. Certainly not to Alexis. He couldn't seem to stop himself.

Now that it was out there, he wanted to take it back. Because Martina was looking at him with pity. He wanted her to *like* him, not pity him.

And, now that he thought about it, how pathetic was that? Here he was, trying to get his interior designer to like him because so few other people did. If she pitied him, he deserved it.

"I don't mean to pry," Martina said, "but have you talked to Alexis? Maybe if you—"

"I don't want to talk to Alexis. And I don't want to talk *about* Alexis." He picked up another french fry and popped it into his mouth. "So, what do you do when you're not working?"

"You invented a dating app," Martina said. "Have you tried—"

"Have I tried my own app? That's kind of problematic given my high profile." *And my high income,* he thought. He didn't want to be targeted by someone looking to use or manipulate him—though that's what had happened anyway with Alexis. He changed the subject. "This tartar sauce is really good. How's your salad?"

BY THE TIME Chris had taken Martina back to Cooper House and she'd picked up her car, she knew a few important things about him.

One, he was lonely as hell. Two, his love life was a mess. And three, he was living a lifestyle that didn't fit him.

Cooper House wasn't the real Chris Mills. The Mustang with its duct tape and its primer spots—that was a lot closer.

So what the hell had he been doing with a woman like Alexis?

And, for that matter, what was he doing living in an opulent

Victorian mansion, when what he really wanted was his action figures and the mess of his computer desk?

How had he gotten to this place in his life, a place where he was playing the part of a rich man, a part he was ill-suited to portray?

THAT NIGHT, it was Martina's turn to cook. Since she was putting a certain amount of work into it, making a butternut squash risotto recipe she'd found online, she'd invited Bianca, TJ, and TJ's son, Owen, to join them. After Bianca had told Martina how overwhelmed she was with the pregnancy and the demands of her job, the least Martina could do was feed Bianca's family for one night.

By seven o'clock, the risotto was on the stove, and Martina had assigned Owen, who'd just turned thirteen, to stir it while she cut vegetables for a salad. Sofia and Benny had poured themselves glasses of white wine and were loitering in the kitchen, and TJ and Patrick were drinking beer in front of the television. Bianca, the best cook of the four sisters, stood by with a glass of sparkling water. Martina was certain Bianca was restraining herself, with some effort, from critiquing Martina's culinary skills.

Instead of criticizing her sister, Bianca focused on her stepson. "Owen? Sweetie, keep stirring."

"I am." The boy peered into the pan. "It's not runny anymore. All the liquid got soaked up."

"Great. Then—" Bianca began.

"That's perfect." Martina cut off Bianca in an effort to avoid letting her sister take over the cooking. "Just add another ladle of broth to the pan and keep stirring."

Owen, whose new teen status had come with a growth spurt that had made his arms and legs look too long for his body, did as instructed. "This is kind of fun," he said. "Bianca never lets me cook at home."

"You want to cook?" Bianca looked at him with surprise.

"Well ... maybe."

"*Hmm,*" Bianca said.

Martina had known it wouldn't be long before someone brought up Chris. She was right—it happened before she even got the meal on the table.

"So, how's the cute rich guy?" Benny asked, sipping her wine.

Martina did think Chris was cute, and the fact that Benny did, too, gave her unexpected pleasure. She would have to analyze that later.

"You mean Chris Mills?" she asked, feigning innocence.

"You know more than one cute rich guy? Wait, you probably do," Benny said. "I mean, there's the whole Delaney clan. That's a lot of eye candy in one family of rich people."

"Yes, she meant Chris Mills," Sofia put in. "You were at his place today, right?"

"I was." Martina diced a tomato and put it into the salad bowl.

"So?" Bianca prompted her. "Was it all fabric swatches and curtain measurements? Or did you get the story on him and his girl-friend?" Bianca leaned on the countertop on her elbows the best she could with her belly in the way.

Martina sliced a cucumber and slid the pieces from her cutting board into the salad bowl. "We did discuss that a little. At lunch." She kept her voice as casual as possible in the hope her sisters wouldn't make more out of it than it was.

Of course, they did make more out of it than it was.

"At lunch? You went to lunch with him?" Benny's eyes widened. "You had a date with a mogul and you're just now mentioning it? Jeez, you know how to bury the lead."

"It wasn't a date. It was just ... lunch." She kept her eyes on the salad, kept her hands busy. "We went to Duckie's. It was nothing."

"Oh. Duckie's. That's pretty casual for a date," Sofia agreed. "Did *he* suggest Duckie's, or did you? Because if he wanted to go some-where nicer and you nixed it ..."

"He suggested it," Martina said. "And it wasn't a date! He felt bad about me having to witness the whole Alexis fiasco, so he wanted to take me to lunch to make up for it."

"There were a few times I inconvenienced my drug rep," Bianca remarked. "I've never taken him out to lunch to make up for it."

"Your drug rep is sixty and bald. And married," Sofia pointed out.

"He's got a certain charm," Bianca said.

"I heard that," TJ called to them from where he was seated on the sofa. "You're carrying my baby. You're not going out with your drug rep."

"Fair. But disappointing," Bianca said.

"Can we get back to Martina's date?" Benny demanded.

"It wasn't a date." Martina carried the bowl of salad to the table and set it down. "It was just ... fish and chips. And a salad. Nothing more."

"Fine. So, what happened on this non-date?" Sofia asked.

Martina stalled by going over to where Owen was still stirring the risotto. She checked the rice, looking for residual moisture, checking the texture and the seasoning. "This looks good. Thanks, Owen." She took the pan off the heat and transferred the risotto into a big ceramic bowl.

Part of her didn't want to talk about it, and part of her did. There was a lot about her exchange with Chris that was confusing her—a lot she needed to sort out. And maybe her sisters could help her do that. On the other hand, she didn't want them making assumptions or ribbing her.

In the end, her need to sort things out won. As they all sat down at the table to eat, she launched into it.

"Alexis is gone. And he seems lonely. Which is weird, because as far as I could see, they didn't even like each other very much." Martina passed the risotto to Patrick, who was sitting between her and Sofia. "When I asked him about her, he mostly changed the subject. But he did say the only reason he hired me in the first place was to get her to stay."

"How hot is she?" TJ wanted to know. "She must be pretty hot if he was willing to do all that."

"She is," Martina admitted. "But that's not the point."

"So, what does that mean for the job?" Bianca wanted to know. "If he was only doing it for her, and she's gone ..."

"It's still on," Martina said. "But now it's different. He wants me to forget the things I was going to do for Alexis. The big dressing room? The expanded master suite? It's over. Now he wants me to redesign the kitchen to look less like it belongs in a five-star restaurant and more like it belongs in an authentic Victorian house. Which I can't wait to do."

"And which, I'm assuming, Alexis would have hated," Sofia put in.

"Right," Martina went on. "And it really seems like it's for him this time. Like he's the one who wants it. Before, he was so disengaged from the whole thing he didn't even care who he was hiring." She shook her head. "It's like he's unplugged from his own life. I mean, he picked my name out of a magazine without learning anything about me. Who does that? Especially for a house like that?"

It was a small speech, and now that she was done, she waited for everyone's responses.

"It seems like you've given a lot of thought to his love life," Patrick said. "Not that I'm judging. It's just ... that's more personal analysis than you'd expect from your interior designer."

"He's not wrong," Bianca said.

"I don't know. It's just ... I want to help him." Martina looked at her plate and not at her family.

"Oh, no," Benny groaned.

"What's that supposed to mean?" Martina was indignant.

"It's like the time you brought home that stray dog. The one with the fleas and the mange," Benny said. "And then you spent a small fortune on vet care for him just to give him to the neighbor. This sounds like that. But with a rich guy. And with emotions instead of mange."

"It's emotional mange," Sofia said.

"Exactly." Bianca pointed one finger at Sofia.

"Nobody has emotional mange," Martina insisted. "And I'm not going to ... to take him to the vet and then give him to the neighbor."

"Maybe you want to get him a nice grooming and a flea collar and keep him for yourself," Benny suggested.

"Can we talk about something else?" Martina said.

"This risotto is great," TJ said. "But the dinner conversation is a little weird."

10

———

Chris tried not to think about Alexis—or about women in general—over the next few days. Clearly, he needed something to fill the empty time now that he'd sold his company and didn't have a job to go to. Of course, there would eventually be a new business enterprise, a new app, a new ... something. But for now, he needed a project.

He'd been neglecting the Mustang sitting in his garage until he'd taken it out with Martina. Being in the car had felt good. Being in it with Martina had felt even better, but that was something to think about another day.

For now, he would think about the car.

He'd told Martina he was restoring it himself, but the fact was, he hadn't done anything with the car since he'd bought it. It had always been a project for another day.

Why not now? What was stopping him? What else did he have to do?

He didn't know much about restoring cars, but at the moment, he had plenty of time to learn.

As Martina had pointed out, he could hire someone to do it—

someone who could bring the car back to its full glory. But what fun would that be?

Standing in his garage on a bright, chilly morning, assessing the car, he decided to pick one small thing and start with that. Otherwise, the job would seem overwhelming.

Because he was standing near the passenger side door, that was what he chose as his first task. The door had a dent that prevented it from opening and closing without the screeching, scraping sound of metal on metal. So, he would replace the door panel.

That seemed doable.

Thinking about the car made him think about the last time he'd driven it, which made him think about Martina.

He wasn't sure thinking about Martina was a wise thing to do—after all, he was fresh out of a troubled relationship and therefore unlikely to make good romantic decisions—but he found himself doing it anyway.

She was different than the women he usually went out with. Very different. The women he usually went out with were like Alexis, and that hadn't worked out as well as one might hope. Maybe a little change was good. Maybe a little change was just what he needed.

No. You've been stupid with women. Maybe figure out how to stop being stupid before you jump into something again.

No doubt, he was giving himself good advice. But how likely was it that he would take it? He was at a place in his life when he needed change. A new project, a new focus, a new direction that would take him into his future.

Why not a new relationship?

Because you keep screwing up relationships, asshole. You need to figure out why. You need to take some time.

He closed the garage door, went inside, and headed to his computer to research how to replace a car door panel.

～

MARTINA HAD A LOT TO DO. She had to work on the schematic design for Chris's kitchen so she could present it to him for his revisions and approval. She had to check in on projects already in process; two were in the construction phase, and she had to monitor them. And she had to work on her assignment for Sofia's wedding: the bridal shower.

She didn't have time to obsess about Chris Mills or to visit pieces of property she couldn't afford to buy. Still, she found herself doing both.

Martina was a born multitasker, so it was no great feat for her to obsess about Chris at the same time as she was viewing the Maxwell Hall property on Lodge Hill.

It didn't take much time to drive from Happy Hill to Lodge Hill—given Cambria's small size, it didn't take much time to drive anywhere from anywhere else. But she used the few minutes to think about the questions of why Chris and Alexis had broken up; why they had been together in the first place; what mistakes, exactly, he was making in his personal life; and how he might fix them. With her help.

She was still pondering all of that as she parked her car in front of the property, located in a woodsy neighborhood of single-family homes, many with a funky, working-class vibe.

Martina already knew the Realtor, a perky, attractive woman in her early forties who worked out of an office on Main Street.

Riley Whittaker's car, a late-model Volvo, was parked at the curb when Martina arrived. As Martina parallel-parked her Prius, the Realtor got out of her car and waited with a polished, professional smile already in place.

"Good morning," Riley chirped as Martina approached her. "Will your client be meeting you here?"

"There's no client this time," Martina said. "It's just me."

A vertical line formed in the center of Riley's forehead. "Oh. If you're looking to renovate a place for yourself, I think you could do a lot better than this property. It's a complete teardown. You'd have to—"

"I'm not looking to do anything in particular." Martina kept her voice light. "I just wanted to see it."

"Should we talk about your budget? The land alone—"

"I just want to take a look, that's all." Martina tried not to show the mounting frustration she was feeling at the way the woman was presenting the property—as though the house itself were nothing but a pile of garbage waiting to be hauled away. "I'm not ready to talk budget."

"All right." Riley's perfectly painted lips curved into a practiced smile. "I've got the key right here. Let's take a look."

WHEN MOST OUT-OF-TOWNERS thought about Cambria real estate, they thought about the oceanfront homes of Marine Terrace or Seaclift Estates, with their tiny lots and expensive houses—tide pools, barking sea lions, and frolicking otters just beyond the front windows.

Lodge Hill was another species entirely.

If you wanted a house surrounded by trees, frequented by wild turkeys and deer, and away from the chilly winds that buffeted the oceanfront properties during much of the year, Lodge Hill was the place to look.

The Maxwell Hall property—which, in fact, hadn't been in the Hall family for a long time—sat atop a woodsy hill overlooking a nature preserve. Riley and Martina walked up an unpaved track, past a fallen pine, and to the house, dirt and pine needles crunching under their feet.

"I should have worn different shoes," the Realtor said, wincing a little as she made her way up a cracked concrete pathway to the house.

Martina stopped and took a good look at the building. Hard angles in metal and glass. The roofline jutting out sharply to shade the redwood deck. A variety of materials—stone and redwood, steel and concrete—forming the geometric shapes that gave the house its modern edge.

"Wow," she said.

"I know." Riley made a face, as though she'd smelled something bad. "It's a wreck."

Objectively, she was right. The deck had collapsed in places, and a strip of yellow CAUTION tape was stretched across the steps leading to it. The largest of the front windows was broken, leaving the interior open to the elements. From here, Martina could see a bird's nest under the eaves, and to her eye, the whole place was tilted slightly, as though the earth beneath it had shifted.

"It's been empty for more than twenty years," Riley went on. "Of course you know it's a Maxwell Hall. Hall himself lived here after he stopped working, and then, when he died, the place just fell to ruin. An investor bought it five years ago, but I guess his plans have changed, so ..." She gestured toward the west and the forest preserve beyond. "If someone wanted to tear down and rebuild, the view would be spectacular."

Martina's first instinct was to express the horror she was feeling at the suggestion of tearing down the house. What kind of monster would destroy an architecturally significant structure to build some new stucco-covered monstrosity? But there wouldn't have been much point to that, so she stayed silent on the matter.

"Can I see inside?" she said instead.

"Of course." Riley clutched her keys like a weapon against whatever they might find inside. "The front entrance isn't safe. We'll have to go around back."

IT REALLY WAS A GLORIOUS WRECK.

They'd had to pick their way through overgrown grass, ferns, and wildflowers to get to the back door. But now that they were standing inside what used to be the living room, Martina thought the effort had been worth it.

"Incredible," she murmured.

"I know." Riley's dry tone indicated she'd taken the comment differently than Martina had intended it. "Can you believe what's happened to this place? You'd think the family would have done something with it after Maxwell Hall's death, but ... I guess there's no accounting for what rich people do."

The house hadn't been occupied by its owner in years, but it *had* been occupied—by local wildlife and, from the looks of the food wrappers and discarded blankets tossed around the room, by at least one squatter.

But that hadn't been what Martina was referring to when she'd said the place was incredible. If you could look past the damage and the mess, if you could ignore the smell of mildew and the spiderwebs spanning the corners of the ceilings, you could imagine how the house had once looked.

It was small, but the huge windows looking toward the forest, the high roofline with its sleek lines and heavy beams, the fireplace stretching toward the ceiling in clean and spare concrete block transported Martina to a time when the house had been new and exciting. When it had been a thing to treasure and not to tear down.

"This space is amazing," Martina said in wonder.

Riley let out a barking laugh. "What, this? Oh, I doubt anyone's going to want to put in the kind of money it would take to renovate it. For one thing, it's far too small. People these days want space and luxury. This place is worth more as a pile of rubble than it is as a house."

Riley saw the look on Martina's face and realized she hadn't been joking. "Oh ... I know you're an interior designer, but—"

"I want to see the rest," Martina said.

The Realtor looked bewildered but resigned. "All right. Suit yourself. But you'll have to go to the second floor by yourself. I'm not taking a chance on those stairs."

"My God, you should have heard how she was talking about it. You'd have thought it was a pile of garbage instead of a significant piece of architecture!" Martina told Benny that evening as the two of them were standing in the kitchen, Benny with a bottle of Coke and Martina with a cup of green tea. Benny had just gotten home from work, and Martina had been glad to have someone to tell about her day.

"But it kind of *is* a pile of garbage," Benny said. "At least, that's what I've heard. Broken windows, trash ..."

"Trash can be cleaned up," Martina said stubbornly. "Broken windows can be fixed. It's not just a Maxwell Hall house. It's Maxwell Hall's own house! Doesn't that mean anything? He was one of the most significant architects of his period. That's worth something!"

"I suppose." Benny took a good-sized slug of her cola. "But what can you do about it? Oh, jeez. You're not planning to buy it, are you? Do you have a winning lottery ticket we don't know about? Because you borrowed twenty dollars from me last week, and if you do, I want it back."

"There's no lottery ticket." Martina frowned. "And, no, I'm not going to try to buy it. I don't have that kind of money. And even if I did, the cost of making the place habitable would be ... Well. It's crazy to even think about it."

"And yet I sense you're thinking about it."

Martina held her mug in both hands, as if to warm them. "I really want to save it."

"Speaking of saving things ... how are things with the mangy mutt?" Benny grinned.

"I don't have a plan yet," Martina said. "For the property or for Chris. But I'm going to save that house. And ... I really want to help the guy." She couldn't bear the thought of him lonely, sad ... so much like the Hall house, but without the spiders and the smell.

"Hell, I'll go out with him," Benny said. "I'm sure I can make some time between all of the other attractive billionaires I'm seeing."

Martina froze and stared at Benny. Then a slow grin spread over her features.

"Wait. You know I was just kidding, right?" Benny said.

"I know you were. But that doesn't make it any less of a great idea."

"No, that's ... no." Benny shook her head and made a shooing gesture with one hand. "I'm not going out with Christopher Mills."

11

M artina let it go, then brought it up again a week later.

She and Benny were sitting at a window table at Jitters on a Saturday morning, each of them with a hot beverage and one of the coffeehouse's signature scones. A light rain created droplets that ran down the window in slow, lazy patterns.

"Why not? You're not seeing anyone. He's not seeing anyone." To Martina, it seemed like the perfect solution to Chris's obvious sadness. Not to mention the fact that Benny hadn't had a date in a while.

"Because. He's a gazillionaire. I wouldn't even know what to say to a guy like that. He should be dating one of the Kardashians. I'm just, you know. Me."

"He's already dated the Kardashians. Well, not the actual Kardashians. But women like them. And it hasn't worked for him. He needs someone real." Martina stirred a packet of stevia into her chamomile tea and took a sip. "Plus, you said he was cute."

"He is cute, in a *guy next door, I have no idea how I got to be a tech mogul* kind of way. But that doesn't mean I want to be fixed up on a humiliating blind date with him. Why don't you date him? You're real."

The idea of going out with him herself had occurred to Martina more than once. Something about the contrast between his wealth—and, therefore, his power—and his emotional vulnerability tugged at her. She'd felt a connection with him, like she'd glimpsed of a part of him that was honest and true. But she was working for him, and that complicated things. And he'd just ended a relationship with a woman much more beautiful and glamorous than Martina could ever hope to be, and that complicated things further.

But that didn't mean she could just stand by and do nothing when she knew she could help him. If she could get Chris and Benny together, she'd be helping two for the price of one. How could she go wrong spreading love and joy to two people who needed it?

"I'm working for him," Martina reminded her sister. "There are too many ways that could go sideways. And anyway, why not? When was the last time you dated someone?"

"I think it was about the time the Yosemite supervolcano was rising through the earth's crust."

"Exactly. What would it hurt to go out with him? You're the one who suggested it."

"I was kidding."

"Well ... I'm not."

Martina could see Benny was thinking about it. She was starting to crack. Of course, no woman wanted to accept the idea of being fixed up on a blind date without at least making a token protest. But now that Benny's objections had been registered, she was softening—Martina could see it in the set of her jaw, the tilt of her lips.

"Okay, so ... how would it work?" Benny asked. "How would you set us up?"

"I don't know yet. But you'll let me do it? You'll let me try?"

Benny shrugged, then allowed herself a grin. "Sure, go for it. Who am I to turn down a date with a super rich, kind of hot guy? Even if he *is* relationship-challenged."

"There you go." Martina felt elated at the idea that she might bring her sister and Chris together. Under that, though, she felt something else—something she might have recognized as jealousy if she'd looked closely enough.

MARTINA CAME up with her plan the next day. She would call Chris and ask him to meet her for dinner, saying she wanted to show him the schematic design for his kitchen remodel. She'd bring Benny along on the pretense that Benny wanted to ask him about creating an app to teach kids about sea life. Halfway through the appetizer, Martina would get a call on her cell phone about some "emergency" that needed her immediate attention. She'd leave, and Benny and Chris would have dinner together. Alone.

Benny would have to take it from there, and if it worked, it worked. If it didn't, at least Martina would know she'd tried.

In the meantime, she had to finish the schematic design, partly to give her ruse some legitimacy, and partly because it was, after all, her job. She also had to figure out what to do about the Maxwell Hall property. She couldn't afford to make an offer on it, but she had to save the house from being torn down.

She got settled on the sofa on Sunday morning with her laptop, her sketches of Chris's kitchen, and her notebook. As she worked on the Cooper House project, she periodically clicked over to the Hall property listing on Zillow.

There had to be some way.

She had a lot to think about, and she hadn't even started work on Sofia's wedding shower yet.

First things first: Chris's kitchen and his personal life. Both of them, she was sure, could be whipped into shape.

CHRIS WAS UNREASONABLY pleased when Martina called to ask him to dinner. He'd just spent the Christmas holiday alone, watching *It's a*

Wonderful Life on TV and drinking too much Scotch, and it felt good
to have something social to look forward to.

Yes, she'd presented it as a business dinner—she wanted to show
him her initial plans for his kitchen. Still, she could have done that at
Cooper House. She wanted to do it over dinner, and that was social. It
was friendly.

He wanted to be friendly and social with Martina—more so the
more he thought about it.

And he thought about it a lot out in his garage in the cool of
midmorning, working to disassemble the passenger side door of
his car.

Chris had never worked on cars as a teenager. He'd never taken
auto shop, and he'd never bought a beater and painstakingly coaxed
it into shape in his parents' driveway.

He'd built a computer from scratch when he was seventeen, but
never a car.

He was probably crazy trying to restore the car himself now,
considering his lack of experience, but he needed a project, and
besides, what was the worst that could go wrong? If he failed, he
could use one of his three other cars while he hired a professional to
fix what he'd broken on the Mustang.

The project was supposed to distract him from his loneliness
since Alexis's departure and from his more and more frequent
musings about Martina, but it was doing neither. There was too
much time to think while doing a job that was mostly physical, rather
than mental, in nature.

Is she seeing anybody?

That was one of the main things on his mind as he sat sideways in
the passenger seat of the car, working to unscrew the arm rest and
remove it from the door.

*I'd be surprised if she's not seeing anyone. And if she is, then what the
hell am I doing thinking about her?*

On the other hand, if she was dating someone, who was it likely
to be? Some local who worked at the grocery store, maybe? A guy
with a dairy farm? Surely he could compete with that. Surely—

"Damn it." His screwdriver slipped and smacked his leg. That was going to bruise.

He focused again on his task—or tried to.

Okay, so if she's seeing someone and it's not serious, I can deal with that. Gotta find out, though.

That was one thing. And another was figuring out why he kept failing with women—why it started out well, then ended with yelling, name-calling (he'd been called names that made him marvel at their sheer inventiveness), and the inevitable leaving.

What was the point in starting something with Martina if it was going to end with her throwing a vase at his head?

Shit. Shit. He'd had to pull the door handle harder than he'd intended in order to get it off, and it had bent in his hand. He looked down at the piece he was holding and made a mental note to order a new one.

He'd invented a dating app, for God's sake—one that had made him a fortune and had brought thousands of couples together. It seemed criminally unfair he couldn't manage to find someone for himself.

Well, to be accurate, he'd found plenty of women for himself—just none who made him happy.

So what if I date her and it doesn't work out? So what? We'll have some fun for as long as it lasts. What's the harm?

But that was a steaming pile of horseshit, and he knew it. Every time one of his relationships failed, he felt less confident, less capable—less like himself. He needed a win. He needed something to work out in his personal life. And if he dated someone new, whether it was Martina or someone else, he needed it to be reasonably healthy, even if they both ended up walking away. If it ended, he needed to feel it had been positive and worthwhile, not a giant train crash with flames and twisted wreckage.

Was that so much to ask?

He'd watched a YouTube video about how to do the job he was attempting, and the next step was to take off the interior door panel. He set to work with a screwdriver, trying to pop the clips that held the panel to the door. The video had warned him not to rip the clips out of the backing of the door panel, but ... *fuck.* There went one of them.

This is hopeless. Not just the car repair, but the repairs to his personal life. It all seemed impossible.

It will be if you can't find your balls, if you can't muster up the guts to even try.

So, he'd try. He'd keep working on the car, and he'd meet Martina for dinner.

At least there was very little danger of an actual train crash. That was something.

12

The dinner was scheduled for that night at The Sandpiper. Benny and Martina were to meet Chris at seven p.m., and by seven thirty, Martina would be gone, Benny and Chris would be sharing a nice bottle of wine, and her plan would be underway.

"What am I supposed to wear? My diamond tiara is being cleaned." Benny fretted in her room as she got ready for the dinner. She'd called Martina in to help her choose an outfit, but Martina's style was so different from Benny's it hardly seemed like she was the woman for the job.

"Wear whatever you'd normally wear on a date," Martina told her. "Try not to think about him as rich. Think of him as just ... you know. A guy."

"Trying not to think of him as rich is like trying not to think of a Bengal tiger as a vicious predator. You can think of it as a nice kitty all you want, but it's still going to chew your face off."

"Nobody's going to chew your face off," Martina said soothingly. "Ooh. Speaking of tigers, though, try this." She pulled a low-cut tiger-print sweater out of Benny's closet and paired with a black pencil skirt. The sweater wasn't something Martina would wear, but it was pure Benny, and authenticity seemed like the best approach.

Well, except for the fact that the whole thing was a ruse.

"Really?" Benny peered at the sweater.

"Sure. It makes your boobs look great."

"It does," Benny agreed. "Give me that." She snatched the sweater out of Martina's hands.

With Benny's wardrobe sorted out, Martina turned her attention to her own clothing for the evening. Though it hardly mattered, since she'd be leaving half an hour into the dinner.

Still, she wanted to look nice, as a matter of simple professionalism. She was going to be showing him the kitchen plan, after all. That part of the evening was real. She had to look like she'd put some care into her appearance.

She went into her room and picked out a maxi dress with a blue and white tie dye print, a flowing skirt, and a low neckline. She paired it with sandals, a turquoise and silver necklace, and a matching bracelet. She wore her hair loose, flowing in waves down her back.

"You've got to be kidding me." Benny scowled at Martina when they both came out of their rooms ready for the evening.

"What?"

"You're wearing that?"

Martina looked down at herself, confused. "What's wrong with it?"

"Other than you looking like some kind of granola-eating, tree-hugging, organic hemp-wearing goddess?"

"What? I—"

"What is the point of you setting me up on this date if you're going to look hotter than I do?"

"But—"

Understanding dawned on Benny's face. "Unless you're *trying* to look hotter than I do."

Martina waved her hands helplessly. "But you do look hot! You look smoking hot!"

"Yes, I do." Benny smiled slyly. "I really do. But you? You're about to sear a hole in the floorboards. You like him."

"What? I do not. I mean, yes, I like him in the sense that he seems like a very decent person who needs a little help finding someone to share his life with. But that doesn't mean—"

"You do. You like him. Otherwise, why did you pull out the big guns? Because that dress"—she pointed one finger at the garment in question—"is the big guns."

At that moment, Sofia and Patrick came in the front door. He'd picked her up from work on his way home from the college, and they both looked tired after a long day.

Patrick's eyes went to Benny first. "Oh. You look nice. Where are you—" His gaze fell on Martina and he stopped in midsentence. "Wow."

"See?" Benny hooted triumphantly. "See? What did I tell you? You're being hot on purpose. Don't deny it."

"What is going on here?" Sofia wanted to know. "What did I miss?"

Benny filled Sofia in on the plan, including how Martina was threatening to disrupt the whole scheme through her excessive hotness.

"And so I ask you," Benny said, in conclusion, "why my sister here would intentionally upstage me, unless she wants to bag Mr. Rich Hottie for herself."

Sofia considered that. "She's got a point."

"I do not want to *bag* him, as you put it, myself." Martina said. "I just want to look nice! Because The Sandpiper is a nice restaurant, and because I'm going to be there as a professional, and ... What do you want me to do? Wear a paper sack with arm holes cut into it?"

Benny smirked. "It's time to go. Let's do this thing."

"I'm not trying to—"

"Okay. Noted. Spray on your patchouli, or whatever you have to do to finish up, and let's get."

Martina grabbed her bag with her papers for Chris tucked into it and headed for the door, certain her sister was thinking of doing something that didn't conform to the plan they'd come up with.

"You're not going to do anything weird, are you?" Martina asked as they went down the front walk and toward Benny's car.

"Weird? No. Of course not," Benny said. "I promise you, I won't do anything that isn't in everyone's best interests."

Oh, shit. That was as good as a confession. Of what, Martina didn't know. She supposed she was going to find out the hard way.

BENNY'S PRESENCE at the dinner wasn't a surprise. Martina wasn't springing her on Chris as some sort of unexpected bonus. She'd called him in advance and asked if it was okay if her sister came along.

He'd seemed surprised, but not displeased. When she'd said Benny was coming to discuss an idea for an app, he'd been courteous and accommodating.

Of course, Martina hoped that when Chris met Benny, he'd be more than courteous—he'd be interested.

That was what she wanted, after all—for both of these people, one she loved deeply and one she was just getting to know—to find each other and discover mutual happiness.

So, why was the idea of it causing a swirling pit of unease to open in her stomach?

They arrived at the restaurant and got a table near the window with a view of the moonlight over Moonstone Beach. Chris hadn't arrived yet, so Martina and Benny settled in to wait for him.

"Sofia should call me at about seven thirty," Martina said, going over her plan. "I'm going to claim it's an unspecified emergency with a client. If he insists on knowing details, I'll say it's an electrical problem in their new kitchen, and they're insisting I come to attend to it."

"You wouldn't be the one to deal with an electrical problem," Benny pointed out. "You'd call Noah, and he'd send an electrician."

"You know that, and I know that, but does Chris know that?" Martina asked.

"I would think anyone with basic knowledge of, you know, *life* would know that."

A little bit flustered, Martina shrugged. "Well, it doesn't matter. About two minutes after I leave, he's going to understand I set him up. Either it's going to work, or it isn't. This thing isn't going to succeed or fail based on the credibility of my client emergency story."

"I can't argue with that," Benny conceded. "And anyway, if the whole thing goes to hell, at least I'll get to have crab cakes. I love The Sandpiper's crab cakes."

They were still discussing the merits of crab cakes in general, and The Sandpiper's crab cakes in particular, when Martina saw Chris come in and approach the hostess stand.

He was wearing dark slacks and a sport coat over a blue dress shirt with no tie, open at the throat. The other times Martina had seen him, he'd been casually dressed, even a little sloppy, relaxing in his own home or wearing jeans and a T-shirt for a trip to Duckie's. But, damn, he cleaned up well. Freshly shaved and with what looked like a new haircut, he would have looked at home on the cover of *GQ* —or maybe *Fortune*.

She wasn't aware Benny was talking to her until her sister said, "Yoo hoo! Anybody home? Martina, snap out of it!"

"What?" Martina blinked a few times and looked at her sister.

"You want him." Benny pointed one lacquered fingernail at her.

"No, I don't."

"For God's sake. Just admit it. Why did you drag me here if you've got a thing for him?"

"I don't have a thing—" Martina cut herself off in midsentence because Chris had spotted them and was making his way to their table.

The two women stood to greet him, and Chris shook hands with Benny. When he saw Martina, his eyes widened and he stopped— stopped talking, stopped moving, stopped doing anything but looking at her. It only lasted a moment, one brief instant, but it was enough. Enough to send a thrill through Martina. And enough to validate what Benny had been saying.

Benny smirked at Martina as Chris pulled out his chair and sat down.

Okay, so Chris was attracted to her. And Martina had to admit that maybe she was attracted to him, too. But that didn't change the fact that she was working for him. It also didn't change the fact that she wasn't an Alexis and never would be.

Martina gathered herself, took a breath, and reminded herself why she was here. Work. And Benny.

"Shall we order drinks?" she asked brightly. "Then we can get started."

AT FIRST, things went according to plan. They ordered wine, Martina brought out her schematic design for his kitchen, they discussed countertops and appliance placement, flooring materials and cabinetry options.

Their appetizers came—of course, Benny ordered the crab cakes —and Martina gave Chris the story she'd invented about Benny's idea for a marine biology app.

Chris was polite, pleasant, and attentive to Benny, but he couldn't seem to take his eyes off Martina—a fact that escaped none of them. Now that they'd started discussing the app, Martina kept trying to move the conversation—and Chris's attention—to Benny.

At seven thirty, Sofia called. But she didn't call Martina, as expected.

She called Benny.

"What?" Benny asked into the phone, wide-eyed. "I can't come now. I'm at dinner." Pause. "An emergency? Oh. Well, if it really can't wait ..."

A moment later, she ended the call, dropped her phone into her purse, and stood up, grabbing her jacket from the back of her chair. "I'm so sorry. God, I feel bad about this, but ... I have an emergency with the ... the thing I'm doing at the college for the science department. I've got to go."

Martina glared at her sister. "You have a marine biology emergency?"

"I do," Benny said earnestly. "The fish tanks at the lab have algae. It can't wait until tomorrow. I've got to go."

Martina couldn't believe Benny was doing this to her—or that she'd conspired with Sofia to do it. She stood up, grabbed her sister's arm, and said to Chris, "I'll just walk her out. I'll be right back."

When they were out of his earshot, Martina spun Benny around to face her. "Algae? In the fish tanks? You've got emergency algae? Benny—"

Benny just grinned. "Martina, he barely glanced at me, but he couldn't stop looking at you. Stay. Have a date with the man. Enjoy yourself. Eat." Benny let out a little gasp. "My crab cakes!" She hurried back to the table and wrapped a couple of crab cakes in a napkin. Then she headed toward the door.

On the way out, she passed Martina. "If I'm not going to get a hottie rich guy, I might as well have my crab cakes."

MARTINA GATHERED her dignity the best she could and went back to the table. She wasn't sure what she was going to say to Chris to explain the way Benny had fled on what was obviously a manufactured emergency.

"So." He took a sip of his wine once she'd gotten settled. "This was, what? An effort to fix me up with your sister? And the fish emergency, I assume, was somebody making a prearranged call to get her out of it?"

What was she supposed to say? The poor guy thought Benny had immediately disliked him and had fled the scene to avoid him.

There was nothing to do but opt for the truth.

"Uh ... yes and no. Yes, I was trying to fix you up with my sister."

She smiled apologetically. "But if you think she left because she didn't like you, that's not it."

His eyebrows rose. "No?"

"No. She left because ... because she thinks I have a thing for you, and she's stepping away to be noble. Some kind of selfless sister thing, like when Angelica gave Hamilton to Eliza."

"Angelica," he repeated.

"Have you seen *Hamilton*?" The whole speech would be useless if he didn't get the reference.

"Twice."

"Oh. Okay. Good, then." She picked up her napkin, fidgeted with it, then set it down again. She could feel him watching her, though, and it was both uncomfortable and undeniably exciting.

"Martina?"

"*Hmm*?"

"Why were you trying to fix me up with your sister?"

It wasn't the question she was expecting. She was expecting him to ask if she really did have a thing for him. Surely he'd get to that eventually, but for now, this was a much easier one to answer.

"Because you seemed really sad and lonely after the breakup with Alexis. And I wanted to help. And ... and Benny's really great. I know she's got the attitude and the sarcasm, but underneath it all, she's such a wonderful person. I just thought if you got to know her ..."

"I meant, why did you fix me up with your sister if you've got a thing for me?" A slight grin tugged at his features.

There it was: the question.

"I ... never said I had a thing for you."

"No. You didn't. So, let's clear that up. Do you?"

She didn't seem to know what to do with her hands. First they were resting on the tabletop, then they were in her lap, then they were fidgeting with her fork.

"I ... don't find you unattractive." *Terrific. A double negative.* She was being both equivocal and confusing.

"You don't?"

"No."

He smiled, just a little, as though in answer to some private thought. "Well. I don't find you unattractive, either. So, it's good to get that out there."

Hearing he wasn't repulsed by her made a blush rise to her cheeks, and she looked down at her lap in a futile effort to hide it.

"Yep," she said. "Cards on the table, and all that."

"So ..."

What? What was he going to suggest? That they end this whole farce, leave the restaurant, and pretend the ill-fated fixup with Benny had never happened?

"So?" she prompted him.

"So, now that we've got that out of the way, and you've shown me your kitchen plans, and Benny's gone, and we're not lying to each other anymore, will you stay out with me?"

"Stay out?"

"Yeah. I was going to ask if you'd go out with me, but we're already out, so ..."

God, that was cute. She couldn't help giggling. "Yes, Chris. I'd love to stay out with you."

13

A t first, when Chris had realized Martina intended to set him up with her sister, he'd been seriously disappointed. He'd thought Martina wanted to have dinner with him herself. He'd thought she was interested in a relationship with him.

That had been both welcome and exciting. He'd liked her from the moment she'd made him tea from herbs she'd clipped in his garden. Something about that nurturing gesture had spoken to him in places so deeply buried that he dared not look at them.

The idea that she didn't want to be with him herself but was only interested in some ill-conceived plan to rescue his love life was not only a letdown, it was mortifying.

But everything had turned out fine after all. Benny had fled, Martina had admitted she wasn't horrified by his appearance, and now here they were, having something that resembled a date.

It wasn't how he'd thought his evening would go, but he'd take it.

They had been served their entrees and more wine, and they talked and ate, and Chris found himself enjoying himself more than he had in months—maybe years.

"So, tell me how you ended up in Cambria." Martina twirled a noodle from her pasta primavera onto her fork. "I assume you started as a tourist—most newcomers here did. But what brings you here long term?"

He took a sip of wine and considered the question. "Yes, I did start as a tourist. I came down here for a long weekend with a girlfriend about seven or eight years ago. The coastline, the green hills—it was spring, so everything was in bloom—the little shops on Main Street. It all spoke to me. So, when my accountant suggested I buy some real estate as an investment ..."

"Your accountant," Martina put in.

"Right. When he said I needed to buy some real estate, I picked up Cooper House, thinking I'd come here on weekends to unwind, get away from it all—you know, all of that. But I got busy with my company, and I didn't make it down here much."

"But now?"

"Now, I've sold the company, and I don't have to be in the Bay Area for business anymore. I was tired of it. Tired of the traffic, the crowds ... just everything. So I thought I'd come down here to figure out my next move."

"Your next move?" She leaned forward a little, her forearms on the table, and the way she moved toward him gave him a glimpse of cleavage over the neckline of her dress. He almost forgot he was supposed to be talking.

"Ah ... yeah. I'm a little too young for retirement."

He'd also discovered that not working was boring as hell, but he didn't add that. He needed to do something with his time, something useful and challenging. He just didn't know what that would be yet.

"So, what's the next move? What are you going to do?"

"I don't know. For now, I'm restoring my car."

She smiled, and he loved the way the smile reached every part of her face—especially her eyes. Alexis had only smiled with her lips— a calculated gesture meant to signify pleasure. That smile had been no more natural than her breasts. But Martina was different. She was real. Both the smile and, he assumed, the breasts.

"Oh. How's that going? Is it harder or easier than putting together an Ikea dresser? Because I have some experience with that, and I'm telling you, it wasn't pretty."

"I've never put together an Ikea dresser."

"Oh. Of course you haven't."

From the change in her expression, he thought he might have said something wrong, though he didn't know what it was.

WELL, that was a stupid thing to say. Of course he'd never put together an Ikea dresser. He could probably buy Ikea if he wanted to. His dressers were probably handmade by Scandinavian forest elves.

The fact she'd even suggested he might shop at Ikea showed the wide gulf between them. She was someone who had, at one time, bought premade, assembly-required big-box furniture, and he probably had people on hand not only to shop for his furniture, but to place it in his home and polish it daily.

What was she doing here? She was in over her head. She'd never dated anyone with this kind of mind-blowing wealth. What could they possibly have in common? What could they have to talk about? How could they ever relate to each other?

But as he went on about his car and about how he'd gone on the Internet to learn to replace the door—with less than ideal results— she found they were talking to each other just fine. She listened to his story about bending the door handle, and she smiled to imagine him struggling through the steps just as anyone else would. She loved that he wanted to do the work himself, with his own hands. Maybe they actually did have something in common.

The conversation came around to her, and she told him about Sofia's upcoming wedding.

"It's getting closer, and we're not completely ready," she told him. "It was planned years ago as Bianca's wedding, but that isn't helping it to go any more smoothly."

His brow furrowed. "What do you mean, Bianca's wedding?"

She'd almost forgotten that everyone didn't know the story. She told him about how Bianca and their mother had planned the wedding when Bianca was sixteen and in love with a boy who, as it happened, was now her husband. She hadn't married TJ back then, of course—she was far too young, even if he hadn't broken her heart the way he did—but Bianca and Carmela had bonded over the exercise, making binders full of plans: the dress, the cake, the venue, the music, the flowers.

She told him that when Sofia had met Patrick, she'd been unable to move the relationship forward because of her grief over their parents. Using Bianca's wedding plan had allowed her to feel closer to their mother, as though Carmela might somehow be there to watch her daughter walk down the aisle.

Chris rubbed at his chin and considered it. "So, Bianca did marry the guy eventually, but Sofia's the one using the wedding she planned?"

"Well ... Bianca had already given Sofia the binders by the time she and TJ decided to get married. Sofia offered to give the plan back when Bianca and TJ got engaged, but Bianca wouldn't hear of it."

"You still haven't told me how your parents died," Chris said softly.

No, she hadn't. Telling that story clouded her world with sorrow that blocked out any joy she might be feeling, and she didn't want to have her world clouded or her joy blocked. She was having too nice a time being here with him.

"That's not a happy story," she said. "And if I tell it, I'm going to stop having fun. Are you sure you want that? Because I don't."

"I guess not, when you put it that way."

"All right then. Should we get dessert?"

CHRIS LOVED HEARING Martina her talk about her sisters, and he loved the bond they obviously shared.

In contrast, Chris was the only child of a single mother who had worked two jobs to support them. When she wasn't working, she was usually drinking. He had come home from school to an empty house most days, and he'd largely had to fend for himself. He didn't blame his mother for the part about the two jobs. She'd had no choice but to work her ass off for their survival. But he could blame her for the drinking—and he had. He still did.

On one hand, he thought having a sibling or two would have made things less lonely for him. On the other, why should more than one kid have to live through what he had?

He hadn't told Martina that story, but he would one day. Just as she'd saved the details of her parents' deaths for a time when their relationship was not so new, he'd saved the story of his upbringing for another day.

Chris sincerely hoped there would be time for all of their stories: hers, his, the happy ones and the not so happy. He wanted more of this—this sense of being where he was supposed to be with the person he was supposed to be there with. He didn't know if Martina was the woman for him—how could he, this soon?—but he knew that right now, he felt content, and that was rare for him.

Right now, he didn't want anything other than what he had, and that was a novelty.

∼

WHEN THEY'D FINISHED dessert and Chris had paid the check, he walked her outside. He wished they had come to the restaurant together; now that he knew this was a date and not just a dinner to discuss remodeling options and app ideas, he relished the idea of driving her home, walking her to her door, and kissing her tenderly, both of them staying quiet so her sisters wouldn't hear.

But he hadn't known it would be a date, so he wasn't prepared. Instead, he would have to settle for saying goodbye at the door to her car.

Then, a miracle. Martina turned to him and explained they'd

come in Benny's car, and she'd left with it. Could he give her a ride home?

He let out a low laugh. "Was that part of the plan? Her leaving with your only mode of transportation so we'd have to go home together?"

Martina blushed. He loved seeing her blush.

"Now that I think about it, yes. It had to be part of the plan. I'm really sorry. If you need to go—"

"Of course I can drive you home." He put his hand on the small of her back and guided her to where he was parked—the Mercedes, this time, because his Mustang currently didn't have a door.

He opened the passenger side door for her and closed it when she was comfortably inside. Then he walked around to his side, whistling.

Was he really whistling? He wasn't even aware that he knew how.

Martina was going to have to yell at Benny when she got home. Either that, or give her an enthusiastic hug.

She'd thought of everything—including the ride home. Martina supposed it would be awkward as hell if she and Chris had suffered through an awful time together, and now she needed to be in his car for the drive back to her place.

But they hadn't had an awful time. They'd had a lovely time. And now, because of Benny's foresight, the very best part of any date with a new person—the goodbye at the door—had been preserved.

Later, Martina might doubt the wisdom of dating a man like Chris—a man who was so far out of her normal experience and who went through women like used paper towels—but now, she just wondered what it might be like to kiss him.

She hadn't kissed anyone in a while, and she missed it. And there was nothing quite like a first kiss with someone new. That sense of infinite possibility, of discovery. The electricity of that first touch.

And the anticipation beforehand.

During the drive to Happy Hill, Martina was intensely aware of Chris in the car beside her. The drive wasn't long, but she spent it speculating about him: Was he a good kisser? It could go either way. She knew he'd been with a lot of women—glamorous, beautiful ones, judging by Alexis. But something about him spoke of awkwardness and self-consciousness, as though he were still a high school senior wondering about his chances of feeling up his prom date.

She liked that he didn't seem self-assured. She sure as hell wasn't, so it put them on equal footing. He was already in a power position compared to her because of his wealth. It would have been too much if he'd also been a smooth, experienced player when it came to dating.

Martina was so involved in her thoughts that she didn't realize they weren't speaking to each other.

Chris said, "Is everything all right?"

"What?" Martina was jarred out of her reverie.

"Just ... you're very quiet. I wondered if you're okay."

"Oh. Yes! I'm fine. Everything's fine."

"That's good. I'm glad." He reached over, took her hand, and held it as he maneuvered the car along Main Street and toward the hills east of Moonstone Beach.

It felt nice to hold a man's hand again.

Even if hers was sweating a little because of her nerves.

WHEN THEY GOT to the house, Chris parked at the curb, got out of the car, and hurried to the passenger side so he could open the door for Martina.

He wanted to be a gentleman. He wanted to impress her with his manners.

He also really wanted to walk her to the door and kiss her.

The walk to the door went fine. He didn't trip over his feet, and neither of them was attacked by a mountain lion, so that was a plus.

But once they got onto the porch and the big moment came—the moment to act or not act—he lost his nerve.

"I had a nice time." Martina turned to face him. She grinned slightly, signaling she might want to continue having a nice time. With him.

"So did I." He knew this was his cue. Damn it, he knew it. He put his hands gently on her shoulders. Her eyes slid closed and her lips parted. She looked so lovely, so ready for this moment between them.

And then ...

CHRIS PATTED Martina's shoulders companionably. "Well, okay, then. I'd better get going. I'll call you about the kitchen." He turned, walked down the porch steps, got into his car, and drove away.

What the hell?

The curtain in the front window moved, and a moment later, the door opened. Sofia stood in the doorway, her hip leaning against the jamb.

"Hey. So, where's Chris?"

"He left."

"Did you have fun?"

"I thought so. But maybe not."

Sofia's brow furrowed. "How do you not know whether you had fun?"

Martina pushed past Sofia, walked into the house, and threw her purse onto the side table next to the door. "Because, when you have fun on a date, and the guy has fun, he kisses you at the end of it, right? Especially when you're standing there like an idiot, waiting for the kiss with your damned eyes closed."

"Uh oh," Sofia said.

"Yeah! Uh oh! At first I was pissed at Benny—and at you, by the way—for setting me up the way you did. But then he admitted he's attracted to me, and I admitted I'm not repulsed by him...."

"Well, that's a start." Sofia closed the door and came into the living room.

"You'd think so. We ate, and we talked. And then I realized I didn't have a ride home, so by now, I'm thinking, that's good. We'll ride home together, we'll say goodnight at the door ... and at the very least, I'll get a damned kiss after going way too long without being kissed."

"Right. That's good." Sofia nodded encouragingly.

"You'd think so," Martina said again. "But when the moment came, he choked."

"Literally?" Sofia looked alarmed. "Like, with the Heimlich and everything?"

"No, you idiot." Martina scowled at her sister. "Not literally. Though I wanted to literally choke him when he patted me on the shoulders and ran away like I'd threatened to audit his taxes."

"Oh. That's not good."

At that moment, Benny emerged from her bedroom dressed in plaid flannel pajama pants and a Green Day T-shirt. "So? How did it go?"

Martina didn't want to tell the story again, so she sank down onto the sofa while Sofia explained what had happened.

"It's not like I think I *deserve* a post-date kiss," Martina said when Sofia had finished. "It's just that I thought ... after the hand-holding and everything ..." She didn't even feel like completing her sentence. She simply went limp instead.

"And you look good tonight, too," Benny observed.

"I do!" Martina wailed. "But not good enough, I guess. Not as good as Alexis. The woman looks like she should be wearing a thong on the cover of *Sport Illustrated*."

Sofia perched on the arm of the sofa, her arms crossed over her chest. "Actually, I have a theory."

Martina didn't say anything, so she went on.

"I used to date a lot of really hot guys," Sofia said.

"That's not a theory," Benny pointed out. "It's just bragging."

"You didn't let me finish. I used to date a lot of really hot guys, and

I never got nervous about it. It was just ... normal. It was just what I did. But then I started seeing Patrick."

"Patrick's attractive," Martina said.

"You don't have to defend Patrick." Sofia waved off the comment. "I know he's attractive. But he's not attractive in a super obvious, in-your-face way like the others were."

"Okay," Benny said. "Your point?"

"My point is, when we got together, it felt ... different. Scarier. More significant. With the hot guys, it was all about the hotness. It was all surface. It was for show."

Benny looked thoughtful. "I get what you're saying. Chris dates the Alexises of the world, and it's like buying a new Mercedes. It's expected. But it's the Mustang he really cares about."

Martina lifted her head and looked at Benny. "Are you comparing me to a car with primer spots and an oil leak?"

"Sort of," Sofia said.

"She's right, though," Benny said. "I can see it. Maybe he didn't kiss you because he doesn't know how to act with someone who's not playing him for the sake of his net worth."

"Huh. If that's true, then it's a little sad," Martina said.

THIS IS FREAKING SAD.

Chris berated himself as he drove from Martina's house to his own. She'd obviously wanted to kiss him. Why had he failed to come through? He'd patted her, for God's sake. Like she was a cocker spaniel.

He pulled up in front of Cooper House, ran his hands through his hair, and sat in the car for a while, thinking about it.

He'd lost his confidence, that's what it was. You could only fail with women so many times before you started to think you were the problem. And once you started thinking that way, it seemed too risky to make a move on a woman you thought you might really like.

Now, Martina probably believed he wasn't attracted to her. Which was flat wrong. He was so attracted to her he could hardly think when she was around. Which was a problem, because he needed to think.

Specifically, he needed to think about what the hell was wrong with him that he'd acted like such an idiot.

He wished he had someone to talk to about all of it. Someone who could give him some much-needed perspective.

He didn't have many friends in Cambria, since he'd been here such a short time. But he did have one.

14

The next morning, a Saturday, Chris sat across the table from Will Bachman at Jitters, each of them with a mug of hot coffee. The coffeehouse was buzzing with tourists gawking over the charm of the place, locals with little dogs in their arms or in their purses, and the usual crowd of senior citizen bicyclists who'd stopped in after their morning ride. The room smelled like fresh-ground espresso beans and warm scones.

Will, a professor at Cal Poly San Luis Obispo, had been Chris's roommate at Stanford when they were both undergrads. Later, Will had worked as a caretaker at Cooper House while he'd studied for his doctorate. Their friendship had almost ended over a woman, but the woman in question had been out of the picture for some time.

Since then, Will had enjoyed considerable success in romance, having married the woman he loved. Chris hoped he might have some helpful insights to share.

"Do you know Martina Russo?" he asked.

"A little." Will sipped his latte. "I know Patrick Connelly, who's engaged to Martina's sister."

"Okay." Chris nodded. "Okay, good."

"What's this about?"

Chris hesitated. How to describe his exact issue and impress upon Will his urgent need to fix it?

"I went out with Martina last night, and I acted like an ass," he said. "And I want to stop acting like an ass, and ... I think *ass* might be my only mode when it comes to women." There. That put it all on the table. Now they'd see what they could do with it.

"Well, that is a problem," Will acknowledged.

Chris nodded, and they both sat with that information for a while as the noise of the coffeehouse buzzed around them.

"Maybe if you told me the actual nature of the asslike behavior," Will prompted him.

So Chris told him about the date: Martina's initial attempt to set him up with Benny; Benny's double-cross of Martina; the delightful evening that had followed; their mutual admission that they didn't find each other revolting; and the drive home, loaded with expectation and longing that he assumed was mutual.

"So then what happened?"

"Then ... I didn't do anything," Chris shook his head in exasperation at his own ineptness. "I didn't kiss her, even though she was standing there clearly expecting me to. And then I patted her and left."

"You patted her."

"You know, like ..." Chris reached out and gave Will a companionable pat on the shoulder to illustrate.

"Oh, boy." Will's voice was full of dread.

"Yes."

Will sipped his coffee and looked thoughtful. "I don't get it. You've never seemed to have problems with women before. There was Alexis, and Juliette, and before that, Melanie ..." Will winced at the mention of the ex-girlfriend the two men had in common.

"Yeah. And look how all of those turned out," Chris reminded him.

"Well, not all of those breakups were your fault."

"Sure," Chris agreed, "but I'm the common denominator, aren't I?"

It all came down to that. You could break down the issues of who had done what to whom, or who had failed to do what for whom. But in the end, if you were analyzing the relationships, how they'd ended, and what they all had in common, it pointed back to him. He was the one element all of those scenarios had shared.

"Has it ever occurred to you ..." Will stopped himself, seeming to think better of whatever it was he'd been about to say.

"Go on," Chris prompted him. "Has what ever occurred to me?"

"Well ... just ... has it ever occurred to you that before Martina, you kept choosing the same type of woman?"

Yes. It had. Chris had met most of the women at the social functions he attended—usually high-priced fundraisers or parties held for the purpose of professional networking. The women had all either been from wealth or were closely associated with it.

These were women who made personal maintenance a full-time job, spending their time being professionally dressed, styled, and waxed until they looked like they'd been run through a selfie filter— even in person. They were poreless, flawless—no cellulite, no patches of dry skin, no bad hair days, no awkward clothing choices, no skin blemishes, not even a freckle or a stray chin hair. He had to admit, with some embarrassment, he'd been proud of the way they'd looked on his arm—and in his Instagram feed.

Not only had he worked hard to keep these women from leaving him, he'd worked equally hard to keep them from revealing things about themselves that might prompt *him* to leave *them*. He'd actively avoided getting to know them.

At some point, he'd convinced himself the appearance of happiness was more important than the real thing, and he'd paid dearly for it.

Will was watching him carefully. "Chris ... look. I didn't mean—"

"No. It's okay. You're right. I do choose the same type of woman for all the wrong reasons. I was just thinking about that. About why I do that."

"Martina Russo isn't that same kind of woman," Will pointed out.

Maybe that was why he'd lost his nerve when it had been time to kiss her. And maybe that was why it all seemed to matter so much more than it ever had before.

"She's different," Chris said. "She's real."

"Well, she doesn't seem to be half constructed of silicone," Will conceded.

Chris let out a barking laugh. "Okay, I deserve that. But you dated Melinda, too, so ..."

"I know. It wasn't one of my better decisions. Live and learn."

That was what Chris wanted, wasn't it? Not just to live, but to learn. To do better. To grow and to avoid the old mistakes he'd made over and over again.

"So, what do I do now? I like Martina. And it's got to be a step in the right direction that she's not like the others. But ... I don't know how to be with someone like her. I don't know what to do."

Will gave him a wry look. "Listen to yourself. You just told me you don't know how to act around a real, genuine woman who might possibly like you for yourself. You might take some time thinking about how it got to this point. I mean, I would get it if you'd always been wealthy. But you used to be one of the little people, just like the rest of us."

The time when he'd been like everyone else had been only about fifteen years before. A blink of an eye, really. But it seemed so distant it might have happened to someone else.

"Things change, don't they?" he said.

"They sure as hell do," Will agreed.

15

It occurred to Martina that during the date that wasn't a date, she'd never gotten Chris's approval of her schematic design for his kitchen. She'd showed it to him, but then the call from Sofia had come in, and that had derailed any talk of business.

That meant she had to talk to him, but the thought of that was mortifying after the way she'd tipped her face up to him, eyes closed, lips parted, full of eager anticipation, only to have him *pat* her.

Still, work was work, and she was a professional. She had to get his signature on the contract so she could proceed with the next phase of the project.

E-mailing was always less fraught with peril than actually talking to someone, so she sat at the kitchen table with her laptop in front of her and composed a message, keeping it crisp and businesslike.

Chris,

If the schematic design I presented to you at dinner is acceptable, I'll need your electronic signature on the attached document. If you require any modifications, please let me know.

Best,

Martina

There. It was exactly the e-mail she would send to a client whom she hadn't expected to kiss. She just hoped he still wanted to work with her after the way she'd misread the situation and made a fool of herself.

Maybe when he'd said he didn't find her unattractive, that was exactly what he'd meant—he didn't think she would scare small children. She'd simply read more into it than there was.

She hit SEND and tried to think about other things—other clients, other opportunities, other men.

Anything and anyone other than Chris Mills.

As CHRIS READ THE E-MAIL, he peered at it in puzzlement and dismay.

The tone of the message sounded like she was trying to sell him life insurance.

It all had to do with the kiss that hadn't happened, he knew. She'd been so warm, so open, so willing. And now she was either offended or pissed off. Or both.

Nice job, Mills, you dipshit.

He was in his garage looking at the car, which was still missing its passenger side door. It was possible he would need to hire a mechanic to reassemble the door, which had been broken down into an alarming number of pieces.

But he wasn't ready for that yet. He was still determined to try.

He'd been hunting around on his phone for an online tutorial when he'd seen the e-mail from Martina.

He pulled up the documents she'd sent, added his electronic signature, and sent them back. Then he sent her a text. He preferred texting to e-mailing. It was so much more immediate.

I've signed the document you sent. We can proceed with the project as scheduled.

There.

He sent the text and immediately regretted it. The tone of the message had mirrored hers—businesslike and direct—because it had seemed advisable to take her cue on their demeanor toward each other. But he didn't feel businesslike and direct when it came to her. He hadn't felt that way when he'd failed to kiss her, and he didn't feel that way now.

So why was he acting as though she were just another person he'd hired to perform a service?

$$\backsim$$

MARTINA READ the screen on her phone. *Proceed with the project as scheduled?* She'd thought they were developing a personal relationship. Now, she was beginning to think he had a stick lodged so far up his ass that he could taste wood.

Well, that was fine, she told herself. She'd thought maybe something was developing, but it wasn't. So what? There would be other men. There would be other dates, other potential kisses. And he'd signed the document, so she still had the Cooper House job.

Sure, she was attracted to him, but again, so what? He wasn't even that great-looking. The world was full of men who were more handsome than Christopher Mills.

Except, it wasn't about *handsome,* was it? It never had been. It was about the way he occupied space in a room, as though the energy and the light and the very molecules of air were drawn to him. It was about his eyes and the way they held a sadness that made her want to soothe and comfort him. It was about the way he smiled at her as though he knew all her secrets.

It had never been about how he looked—not for her.

She was intrigued, that was all. But she would be intrigued by other men—men who knew when to kiss a woman and when to pat her and leave.

She was still pondering it when her phone pinged with another incoming text message.

I should have kissed you.

She stared at her phone, a delicious tingle running through her. She didn't want to tingle for someone who might not want her. And yet ...

Yes, you should have. She hit SEND and waited, watching the phone.

His answer came a moment later: *Mistakes were made.*

She couldn't help it: a giggle escaped her lips, and she put a hand over her mouth to contain it.

Don't let it happen again, she responded.

Then she waited, thinking, *please. Please.*

Does that mean there will be other opportunities? he asked.

She thought about what to answer, considering and then rejecting a number of responses—some because they weren't flirty enough, and others because they were too flirty and might be the text message equivalent of her standing there fruitlessly waiting to be kissed.

Finally, she wrote: *Only if you've learned from what you did wrong.*

He sent back a smiley emoticon—that was it. Just a yellow circle smiling at her. What was that supposed to mean? Did it mean yes, he'd learned from his error? Did it mean he wanted to see her again? Or did it mean he was amused by their conversation but had no actual plan to pursue anything with her?

"Well, damn it." She tossed her phone onto the table and scowled.

AT THE TIME, Chris had thought sending the smiley emoticon was a brilliant move. It was flirty, certainly. Positive. Friendly, but at the same time, mysterious. It didn't give away too much. It hinted at exciting things to come without prematurely tipping his hand.

But, not long after he sent it, he began to doubt himself. What if sending an emoticon seemed immature? What if she misinterpreted it as lack of contrition for his failures? And then there was the practical aspect: the wordless smiley face had effectively ended the conversation before they had another date planned.

The question of when he might follow up on the hinted promise of the emoticon had been left wide open, with no future potential kiss in sight.

Damn it.

He put down some random part of his car door that he couldn't identify, went to the worktable in his garage, picked up his phone, and stared at it. He'd hoped maybe she'd texted again, giving him another opening. But she hadn't.

The ball was still in his court—he just had to decide how, exactly, to hit it and what kind of spin to put on it.

While he was still holding the phone in his hand, it rang, startling him.

Will's name came up on the screen, along with a photo of his face.

"Have you talked to Martina yet?" Will asked when Chris answered the call.

"We haven't talked, exactly. We've texted."

"You texted."

"Well ... yes." Chris held his head in his free hand as he contemplated his ineptitude. "I sent her a smiley emoticon."

Will was silent for a moment that seemed steeped in judgment. Then: "You're falling apart, man."

"I know." Chris sighed. "I know it."

He was going to need a new plan, something other than what he'd done with his previous girlfriends. A new plan, meaning Martina wanted real interaction, not just the appearance of perfection. A new plan, meaning he couldn't rely on his bank account to make him more attractive. A new plan, meaning he would actually have to get to know Martina in a way he'd never really known the other women in his life.

That scared the hell out of him.

"I'm not sure I'm up for this." He massaged his forehead with his fingertips.

"I'm not sure you are, either," Will said.

16

Martina didn't know what the smiley face meant, and she didn't have time to think about it. She had a lot to do. She needed to work on the final, more detailed plan for Chris's kitchen; she had to move her other projects forward, including two currently in the construction phase; she needed to work on her assignments for Sofia's wedding; and she needed to come up with a plan for how she was going to buy the Hall property —an idea she hadn't yet given up on despite her lack of money.

The Monday after the text exchange, she got an early start, eating a quick breakfast of muesli and yogurt before grabbing her bag and heading to a house on Park Hill where she and Noah were working on expanding a client's master bathroom.

The house, which had been built in the 1970s, had an exterior of green stucco with a steeply arched roof and a front deck that had seen better days. She would have loved to redesign the whole thing— she could imagine a completely updated exterior with new paint, new landscaping, and a more inviting entryway—but the client only had a budget for the bathroom.

With the homeowner off at work in San Luis Obispo, Noah and

his crew had the front door wide open, dropcloths on the wood floor as they carried old fixtures, flooring, and broken pieces of drywall to Noah's truck to be hauled away.

Martina caught Noah as he walked out of the house carrying an avocado green toilet.

"How's the demo coming?" she asked.

He put down the toilet and straightened up, putting a hand to the small of his back. "Not bad. We got the bathtub and the sink out already. This is the last of the fixtures." He motioned toward the toilet.

"It's green," Martina observed.

"They don't make 'em like that anymore. I'm almost sorry to see it go."

"Really?" Martina wrinkled her nose.

"No, not really. Thing's too ugly even for somebody's ass."

As workers went into and out of the house behind them, Noah updated her on their progress. The demo would be done today, with all fixtures and flooring removed, the wood paneling taken out, and the wall separating the bathroom from a storage closet removed. Tomorrow, the plumber would come to install the pipes so they could build a walk-in shower where the closet used to be.

Noah had hoped he could get the electrician over there tomorrow, too, so he could put in a new exhaust fan and light fixture combo, but the guy had called to say he couldn't make it because his wife was sick.

"Nothing serious, I hope," Martina said.

Noah made a *pffft* sound with his mouth. "Eddie's wife manages to get sick whenever the surf's good at Pismo. Kind of a funny coincidence. When he shows up for work, he's gonna have a nice tan that ends at the neck of his wetsuit."

If Martina were a more controlling person, she'd have given Noah a hard time about it, insisting to know how this was going to affect the timeline for the job and whether he should find another electrician to replace Eddie.

But one of the reasons she and Noah worked so well together was that she let him do his job, and he trusted her to do her own.

Instead of pushing him, she blew out a breath and nodded. "Okay. Well, keep me updated."

"Will do. Meantime, the floor tiles came in. You want to take a look?"

∼

WITH THAT DONE, Martina had intended to go home to start work on the final design for the Cooper House kitchen. Instead, she found herself driving right past Happy Hill and toward the other side of town so she could get another look at the Maxwell Hall house.

When she reached the woodsy parcel Riley Whittaker had shown her, she parked on the street, got out of her car, and picked her way up the overgrown path toward the house. She was trespassing, of course, but she couldn't imagine anyone would care—especially if she ended up making an offer on the place.

Which I can't do, Martina reminded herself.

When she was standing in front of the house, looking at its sleek lines and bold silhouette, she knew she had to think of something. She had to try.

She did have some savings, and she wasn't entirely without assets.

This called for a family meeting.

∼

"... So I thought you could buy out my share of the house, then I could pay rent to continue living here until the Hall house is finished," Martina concluded as her sisters, TJ, and Patrick listened.

The four Russo sisters had inherited the house after their parents had died, and they each owned a quarter of the property. Because the place had a sliver of an ocean view, because it was a historic building, and because the senior Russos had renovated the house so beautifully, even a quarter of the value of the place was a substantial sum.

That sum, along with her savings, would give Martina enough to make a good-sized down payment on the Hall house.

"Oh." Sofia frowned and looked at Patrick as the others considered her proposal.

"What does 'oh' mean?" Martina asked.

"It means this is really bad timing," Sofia said. "We put most of our savings into the wedding. You know Bianca doesn't pay me much —sorry, Bianca—and Patrick's salary ..."

"Right." Martina nodded. She'd known that, but she'd hoped ...

"God, Martina. I can't come up with that kind of money." Benny looked at her sister with regret. "I really wish I could. I'd love to help you, but I've still got my student loans."

"I know. It's okay." Martina felt tears welling up in her eyes, and she willed them to go away. She didn't want Benny and Sofia to feel bad for something that wasn't their fault.

"TJ and I could buy your share," Bianca said. "Couldn't we?" Bianca looked at her husband.

"Maybe." TJ rubbed at the stubble on his chin. "We'd have to run the numbers."

"Really?" Martina jumped out of her seat. She couldn't seem to help herself. Her excitement made sitting impossible.

"Maybe," TJ said again, this time emphasizing the word. "If we look at the numbers and it doesn't make sense for us to do it ..."

"Of course," Martina said. "Of course I wouldn't want you to do anything financially irresponsible."

"But," TJ went on, "it's coastal real estate, and that's never a bad investment. So, I tend to think—"

"Thank you!" Martina launched herself at TJ, who was sitting on the sofa. She threw her arms around him and squeezed.

TJ patted her back and said, "Oh. Ha, ha. Well."

Bianca put her hand on her husband's shoulder and said, "I love you, you know."

"That's convenient, since you're having my baby." He gave Bianca's midsection an affectionate rub.

"Now that we've got that out of the way," Benny said, "how are you going to pay for the renovations? You said the place is a wreck. The Realtor is calling it a teardown. That's not going to be cheap."

"Are you going to be able to get a mortgage?" Patrick's brows drew together in concern. "With the damage to the house ..."

"I won't be able to get a conventional mortgage," Martina admitted. "I'll have to apply for an FHA 203(k)." Because of Martina's work —especially involving homes that needed extensive repairs—she was well aware of the financing options. But her sisters and the men were giving her blank looks. "It's a rehab mortgage," she said. "I can finance the cost of the purchase as well as the costs of repairs. If I qualify."

That was the questionable part. The cost of the property plus the renovations was substantial, and Martina was self-employed. Her business had been doing well the past couple of years, but the decision on the mortgage could go either way.

The Cooper House renovation would help—a lot—if Chris decided to do more than just the kitchen. But she didn't want to count on that, partly because you could never count on what a client might do, and partly because of the personal relationship developing between them. The last thing she wanted was to start dating him, then put pressure on him to continue working with her so she could get approved for the mortgage.

She would just have to keep Chris out of it. She simply wouldn't tell him about her need to improve her financial profile in order to apply for a mortgage. That would be too fraught with complications.

If he continued to hire her to work on his house, she wanted it to be because of her talent and because of his own vision for his home. She didn't want him doing her favors to get her into bed.

If he did, in fact, want to get her into bed. Which she was pretty sure he did.

"So ... this means you're going to move out, right?" Sofia's face had taken on that pink, pinched look it got when she was feeling emotional.

Martina reached out and squeezed her sister's hand. "Eventually, yes. I love it here. Really. Being here after losing Mom and Dad ..."

Now *she* was the one who was probably pink and pinched. "It's just meant a lot. But I want a place I can make my own."

"It makes sense from a business standpoint." Benny was standing with her arms crossed over her chest, looking at Martina appraisingly. "As an interior designer, you need your house to be a place that shows off your style, especially when you're working out of your home. This place shows off Mom and Dad's style, which is great. But it's different than yours."

"Exactly." Martina was grateful Benny understood. "And I need a home office. Spreading my stuff out on the kitchen table just isn't working anymore."

When Bianca had moved out, Martina had considered asking her sisters if she could take over the vacated room, but that hadn't seemed fair to the others, so she hadn't brought it up.

So far, the room had been used mostly to store Patrick's belongings until he and Sofia could afford a place of their own. The space where Bianca's bed used to be was now occupied by U-Haul boxes marked KITCHEN and MISCELLANEOUS. If Martina wanted to use that space, Sofia and Patrick would have to rent a storage unit, and that would set back their efforts to save for their eventual home.

It was better for everyone if Martina figured out something else.

"We'll miss you." Sofia looked like she was on the verge of tears.

"I'll be two and a half miles away." Martina got up from where she was sitting and hugged her sister.

In truth, two and a half miles was going to feel like much more. She and her sisters had grown close since they'd moved in together in the wake of their parents' deaths. They'd needed each other then, when they'd all been gutted by grief, unable to see their way forward in a world that no longer had Aldo and Carmela in it. Being here, in this place their parents had lovingly made, had been a big part of their healing.

But it was important to move forward rather than standing still. Moving forward meant finally buying her own place. And it also might mean a new relationship with a man she found very appealing.

Funny how Chris kept popping into her thoughts even when he

wasn't with her, even when she was thinking about things that had nothing to do with him.

That was probably something to think about.

17

N ew Year's Eve had come and gone, and Chris still hadn't asked Martina out again. Once he did, it could—depending on the criteria you used—be considered their third date. The third date, in his experience, was often the sex date. But he and Martina hadn't kissed yet, so if all went well, it would definitely be the kissing date.

If he could just get up the nerve to ask her.

Okay, yes, he'd had problems with women. But those problems had always been about keeping a relationship going in the long term. He'd never had trouble with the initial phases—asking someone out, negotiating those first dates, the first time getting physical.

So what the hell was his issue now?

He remembered the many times in his career when he'd found himself unable to come up with new, creative ideas, unable to hit on that original concept that could be parlayed into a profitable piece of software. He'd have called it a creative block.

Well, now he was having a similar type of block, this one related to his personal life.

The good news was, in his experience, the worst bouts of creative block were often followed by his biggest breakthroughs.

He thought about all of that as he worked his way through an early morning run on the bluff trail at Fiscalini Ranch. Coastal fog shrouded the landscape in a soft white glow as the surf crashed against the rocks below. Sea birds screeched and cawed, and a squirrel dashed across the path ahead of him. He was feeling loose and relaxed, a pleasant sheen of sweat on his face and body. The contrast between the cool morning air and the heat of his exertion made him feel energized and exhilarated.

This was why he'd come to the Central Coast in the first place—this feeling of being in nature, of being part of the rugged landscape around him. He'd never run until he'd come to Cambria. There'd seemed to be so little reason to go outside in his previous life, before he'd sold his company. Before he'd moved out of the concrete and traffic of the city and found his way here.

As his sneakers pounded the dirt path, his mind kept wandering back to Martina.

The best way out of a creative block, he'd found, was to change what he was doing and try something different. Sometimes all it took was some small variation in his routine, such as going to a different coffee place in the morning or taking a different route to work.

It was all about the patterns. When you changed your pattern, you changed the way your brain processed everything you were doing. And when your brain started processing things differently, sometimes good things happened.

He'd already changed so much, though. He'd sold his company. He'd moved here. He'd broken up with Alexis. He'd finally started working on his Mustang.

What else was there to change?

Only everything about the way you deal with women, dumbass.

Yes, there was that.

Maybe he needed to do the opposite of whatever his instincts told him to do. He could try that and see what happened.

His instincts told him to wait a while longer, then text Martina to feel her out on whether she was amenable to seeing him again. So, he stopped, breathing hard, sat down on a bench overlooking the ocean, pulled his cell phone out of his pocket, and called her.

He didn't wait, and he didn't text her—he *called* her.

She answered on the third ring. It wasn't until then he realized it wasn't even eight a.m. What if she hadn't been up yet? What if she'd been sleeping in? He silently cursed himself for his idiocy. She wasn't going to be in a favorable mood toward him if he'd interrupted some pleasant dream or if—

"Hi, Chris."

Her voice interrupted his thoughts, and he realized if he didn't say something, he was going to seem like a crank caller, especially because he was still breathing heavily from his run.

"Martina? Hello. Ah ... I'm sorry for calling so early. I didn't realize ... I was out for a run, and I hadn't looked at the clock...."

"That's all right." She didn't sound as though she'd been asleep, so that was good. "What's up?"

His heart rate, for one. His anxiety. His fight-or-flight response.

"I was just ... I was wondering if you'd like to come to the house and have dinner with me. Tonight." There. He'd gotten it out. And he'd continued with his strategy of ignoring his instincts. Usually at this stage, he'd take a woman to the most expensive restaurant he could find. Inviting her to his home for a meal was an entirely new approach.

"You called me at seven forty-five in the morning to ask me if I'd have dinner with you?"

He was encouraged that she sounded amused rather than annoyed.

"I didn't realize it was so early. I can hang up and call back if you—"

"I'd love to," she said.

Mixing things up was going pretty well so far.

∿

USUALLY WHEN CHRIS got around to inviting women to his house for dinner, someone else cooked the meal—someone who was being paid to do it. Since he'd resolved to do everything differently this time, he decided to cook the food himself.

The problem was, he didn't know how to cook any more than he knew how to restore an old Mustang.

Still, he was trying with the Mustang, with the help of instructions and YouTube tutorials he found on the Internet. There was no reason he couldn't approach the dinner the same way.

The fact that he didn't currently have a job—or any obligations at all, for that matter—allowed him to focus all of his energy on the task. Once he'd gotten home from his run and had showered, shaved, and dressed, he applied himself to the question of what to cook for Martina.

He settled in at his desk and Googled the phrase, *what to cook for a date night*. The first page of results looked promising—until he noticed most of them involved meat of some kind. Martina didn't eat meat. He tried again, this time typing, *what to cook for a date night vegetarian*.

Okay, better.

Now he was faced with a new problem: since he wasn't a vegetarian himself, he found many of the recipes both odd and offputting.

Cauliflower steaks? Curried tofu? Miso-tahini noodles?

The miso-tahini part was beyond him, but noodles seemed safe. He searched for a good vegetarian pasta recipe. At least he was familiar with pasta. It would probably help if he'd at least, at some point, eaten the type of food he was trying to make.

He was starting to feel good about the idea of pasta until he realized Martina was Italian. Generally speaking, it didn't seem like a good idea for someone with marginal cooking skills to try to impress an Italian woman by making pasta.

The whole thing was like a booby trap waiting to go off.

"I don't know how to cook," he told Will during a desperate phone call.

"And I'm not very good at skeet shooting," Will responded. "But I find it doesn't come up much in my daily life."

"Well, cooking *is* coming up in my daily life. Today, specifically. I invited Martina over for dinner, and I want to make the meal myself. Only, I don't cook."

"That's a problem."

"Exactly," Chris said.

"I know some good caterers if you want to—"

"No. I'm doing this. I just ... I don't know where to start."

Will was silent for a moment. Then he said, "You really like her."

"Of course I like her," Chris said irritably. "Would I be dating her if I didn't like her?"

"Maybe." Will was unperturbed. "I always got the feeling you didn't really like Alexis. Or Melinda, for that matter."

It was a fair point. He'd liked being with those women because they were attractive and the sex was good, and it kept him from being lonely. Also, he'd liked being seen with beautiful women, had liked it when pictures showed up on social media of himself with his arm around someone who hit a solid nine on the one-to-ten hotness scale.

But had he liked the women themselves? Had he liked talking to them, just being with them when everyone was clothed and there was no one around to see who he was with or what he was doing?

"All right, maybe I didn't like Alexis all that much. Or Melinda. But that doesn't mean—"

"You like Martina, though. Really, truly like her. Because you're putting yourself out for her, and that's not something you usually do."

Chris frowned. "I was going to have Cooper House remodeled for Alexis. How's that not putting myself out for her?"

"You were going to write a check," Will said. "Or several of them, I imagine. But someone else was going to do all the work. This is different. This is *you* doing the work. You like her."

Chris hadn't thought about it in exactly that way, but Will was right. This was different, not just because he was consciously applying himself to the task of acting differently. It was different because Martina was special.

He wasn't ready to say that out loud, though, so instead he asked, "So, what am I supposed to make to impress a vegetarian?"

18

Martina tried not to think too much about her date with Chris. If she thought about it, the whole thing would be too fraught with expectation—she'd be too preoccupied with what might happen at the end of the evening, when he would either correct his failure to kiss her, or he wouldn't.

What if he did? And, just as importantly, what if he didn't? It was all too much to think about, so she spent her day focused on other things.

The Hall house, for one thing.

She didn't want to pressure Bianca and TJ on their decision about whether to buy her share of the family home, but time was an important consideration. She needed to move on the property before someone else did.

If Bianca and TJ did decide to buy her share of the cabin, that would take time. She was pretty sure they didn't have a couple hundred thousand dollars lying around, so they would have to liquidate investments. Then there would be contracts to be drawn up and signed.

Martina hoped by the time all of that was done, it wouldn't be too late. It seemed likely the property would sit on the market for a while, given that the house was uninhabitable. But the land was lovely, and it had an active water meter, so it could go either way.

Sitting at the kitchen table with her laptop, Martina ran the numbers again. She created a spreadsheet with her bank account balances, her debt—which was minimal—her assets, and the likely mortgage payment on the property.

She'd inherited some money from her parents as well as her share of the house, so that would help.

"What are you doing?" Benny looked over Martina's shoulder at the computer screen. Benny was dressed for work, her bag already slung over her shoulder.

"I'm not thinking about Chris," Martina responded.

"Not thinking about Chris requires an Excel spreadsheet?"

"It does this morning." She closed the laptop and looked at her sister. "He called me just after dawn to invite me to his house for dinner."

"Ooh!" Benny plopped into the chair next to Martina, grinning. "Dinner at his place! You know what that means. And this is date three, right?"

"This is not a sex date," Martina insisted. "We haven't even kissed yet."

"Just because you haven't sampled the appetizer doesn't mean you can't dig right into the main course," Benny said.

"It does for me."

Benny nodded. "Fine. But there'd better be kissing. If there's no kissing ..."

"I know. He didn't even *serve* the appetizer last time. Tonight, I'd better at least get a damned bread basket." Martina went with the metaphor, because it seemed apt.

It had been a long time since she'd eaten—metaphorically—and she was pretty damned hungry.

~

THE APPETIZER WAS SERVED right after Martina's arrival, though it was a real, and not metaphorical, appetizer of stuffed mushroom caps. She was hungry—actually, not just metaphorically—and she loved stuffed mushroom caps, so it was a welcome development.

"You made these?" Martina looked appreciatively at a mushroom cap before popping one into her mouth.

"I did." He looked pleased with himself. "I had some help, though. I called my friend Will, and he called his friend Jackson, who's the chef at Neptune."

Martina reconsidered the mushroom caps. "Don't tell me Jackson Graham made these." The mushrooms were good—very good—but they weren't quite Jackson Graham quality.

"No. He e-mailed me the recipe. I did all the work."

It pleased Martina that Chris had made the food himself, especially because he didn't have to. With his money, he could have brought in a chef from France for the occasion.

He hadn't done that, and instead had gone to some trouble on her account, and that made her feel like he was taking this date seriously. If he'd bothered to cook—something he didn't usually do, she was guessing—then he must think this could lead somewhere.

That idea made Martina simultaneously pleased and scared. For one thing, any serious relationship with Chris would be a threesome: her, him, and his money. It was both intimidating and unsettling.

"So, what do you think?" He gestured toward the mushrooms.

"Really good. I love a good appetizer." She couldn't help grinning, thinking of her private joke with Benny.

HE WOULD KISS her sometime tonight. He had to, after his failure to do so the last time he'd had an opportunity. Besides, he wanted to. The wanting to and the needing to combined to make his palms sweat, and that was making it hard to chop vegetables for the ragout.

In the interest of not losing a finger, he put down the chef's knife and moved a couple of feet to where she was standing with a glass of white wine in her hand.

"I was going to do this later, but ..." He hesitated, then put his hands on her shoulders and moved in for the kiss.

Her lips were soft and tasted of chardonnay. She tilted her head to accommodate him, and a gentle sound escaped her as he caressed her mouth with his own.

He wanted more, but not yet. There would be time for that. Usually in a situation like this, if the signs pointed to yes, he would try to get a woman into bed before the main course. But he was doing things differently this time. Taking a different tack.

So, instead of deepening the kiss, he pulled back, enjoying the look of her as she stood there with her eyes still closed, her lips still slightly parted.

"I should have done that last time," he said.

She opened her eyes as though waking from a deep sleep. "Better late than never."

~

THE KISS HAD BEEN VERY good.

The thing about kisses was that they could go either way, and you couldn't know how it would be until it happened.

Bad kisses came in a whole range of awfulness, from the surprise collision of teeth to the unwanted tongue, lips too hard and dry or too soft and wet, or the times when everything seemed technically okay, but the kiss nonetheless left her feeling a vast chasm of nothingness —no passion, no warmth, no desire for more.

But this kiss had that undefinable something, that unknowable ingredient that elevated it from a mere meeting of lips to something transcendent.

It had been gentle at first, soft, tentative, and then had become more assured. As her mouth had fit comfortably with his, something in her body had relaxed and grown warm and happy, and she'd leaned into him without realizing she'd done it.

The kiss had been excellent, and it made her wonder what other excellent things he might offer her.

∼

CHRIS WAS NOT unhappy with how the dinner turned out. Vegetarian ragout over polenta, with a salad and, of course, the mushroom caps. He'd have to thank Jackson Graham; the recipes he'd provided to Chris had been relatively easy to make but looked and tasted as though Chris had far more advanced skills in the kitchen than he did.

Jackson should consider publishing a cookbook: *Date-Night Meals for Men Who Can't Cook,* or something like that. Was there anything similar out there? He'd have to check. It could be a real moneymaker. Paired with one of Chris's dating apps—

"What are you thinking about?" Martina looked at him from across the dining table, a forkful of salad poised above her plate.

"Oh, just … a business idea." He was embarrassed she'd caught him with his mind wandering. He didn't want her to think he wasn't focused on her. It was just how his brain worked.

"Oh." She ate the bite of salad, and he could see by the way her expression changed that she'd taken the comment exactly the way he'd feared.

"I'm not bored," he blurted out.

"Okay."

"I just meant, if you thought I was thinking about business because I'm bored or because I don't want to be here with you, that's not it. When I get an idea, it's hard to turn my mind off. You're probably that way with interior design. Or maybe you're not. But for me …" He was rambling, and he had to force himself to stop.

"I can be that way sometimes." She smiled at him, and he felt relieved. "It's hard to visit someone's house without thinking about how I'd redo the living room."

"Exactly." He took a sip of wine. "You know, I got my best idea while I was losing my virginity."

Martina's eyes widened, and her grin spread. She put down her fork. "Literally at the moment you were having sex for the first time?"

"Literally at the moment." This was probably a bad story to tell a woman he hoped to sleep with, but it was already out there, and there would be no turning back now.

"How old were you?"

"Nineteen. I was a freshman at Stanford, and I was in the girl's dorm room while her roommate was away. MacKenzie Cameron. She was an English major. Really pretty. I couldn't believe my luck."

"Okay, so what was the idea?"

"Well, we were both gamers, and we were both into the same MMORPG...."

She looked at him blankly. "What's an MMORPG?"

"It stands for *massively multiplayer online role-playing game.* Anyway, we were both into this game called DarkSpace, and that's how we ended up talking to each other, through this community of people who played the game. And I thought, *There's no other way a girl like this is going to get together with someone like me.* And that made me think...."

"Oh, my God." Martina put a hand over her mouth. "You had the idea for PlayDate during *sex*?"

Of course she knew about PlayDate, the app that had made him his fortune. It was a damned good app, and all these years later, it remained the thing he was best known for.

"I did. And ... I probably shouldn't have told you that story."

"No, it's a great story," Martina said. "Though I kind of doubt that's the version you've told the media over the years."

A little embarrassed, he looked at his plate instead of at her. "I did tell them I thought of it during a date with MacKenzie, but in the public version, we were at the movies."

"Probably smart," she said.

∾

AFTER DINNER, they left the mess where it was and took their wine into the library, where Chris lit a fire and they sat together on the sofa in front of the fireplace. It had started to rain during dinner, and the sound of rainfall tapping on the windows made the room, with its classic look of dark paneling and floor-to-ceiling bookshelves, feel warm and inviting.

Martina had already decided she wasn't going to sleep with him. At least, not tonight. For one thing, it was far too soon. For another, she'd be lying there wondering what multimillion-dollar business scheme he was cooking up while he was making love to her.

But that didn't mean they couldn't make out for a while before she went home.

They drank a little more wine, making Martina feel loose and relaxed, and then he took her glass from her and put it on the coffee table with his own.

"I liked our kiss earlier," he told her. "I'd like to do it again, if that's okay."

"It is."

He gently lay the palm of his hand against her cheek, then leaned in toward her. He hesitated just a moment, just long enough to extend the anticipation, then took her mouth with his own.

Martina felt a sense of weightlessness, of floating. That was when she knew she might be in this deeper than she'd realized. She'd never felt weightless during a kiss before, but here she was, untethered, as though the world around her had lost its very substance.

She opened her mouth to him, and he deepened the kiss. She put her arms around him, hands splayed on his back. He smelled like the wine they'd been drinking, and some light and spicy aftershave, and something else.... Oh, yes. Trouble. He smelled to her like the very essence of trouble.

He pulled back a little and said her name, and it sounded sensual, erotic on his lips. He threaded her long hair through the fingers of one hand.

"I should go," she said.

She hadn't been aware she was going to say it until it was out of her mouth. Part of her wanted to tell herself to shut the hell up. Why not stay? Why not enjoy everything he had to offer?

But another, stronger part of her knew leaving was the right thing to do. It was absolutely too soon to sleep with him, and that was what she was going to do if she stayed.

If she didn't get out of here now, this moment, not only would she sleep with him, she'd be tempted to follow this yellow brick road so far away from Kansas that she'd never see Auntie Em again.

She said it again, just to steel her resolve: "I ... I really have to go."

"Okay." He nodded and swallowed hard. "Just ... are you going because it was a really bad date and you didn't like the kiss? Or ..."

"I'm going because it was a really good date and I don't want to do anything I'm not ready for."

"Good. That's good." His goofy grin gave Martina all kinds of feelings and urges that were inconvenient for her to be feeling this early in their relationship.

She stood up to go, then leaned down and kissed him, her hand on the back of his neck. "Thank you for dinner."

Even though she was running like hell, that didn't mean she couldn't be courteous.

19

C hris felt pleased with himself the morning after his date with Martina as he went through his routine: shower, coffee, getting dressed, and planning his day.

True, the date had not ended in sex, but he'd been pretty sure it wouldn't, so that was fine. He could wait. The kisses had been exceptional, so he was betting the sex—if it happened—would be worth waiting for.

And it wasn't just the promise of exceptional sex that interested him. He enjoyed talking to her, even if they were talking about something trivial, something that, were he talking to anyone else, would be boring or tedious. Just listening to her voice was enough.

He found himself wanting to tell her things he didn't want to tell anyone else.

Case in point, the lost virginity story.

He could see, in retrospect, it probably hadn't been a good idea to share that particular anecdote with her. When they finally had sex— if they had sex—she'd be wondering whether he was running through a sequence of coding in his brain. (Which, in fairness, he might actually do if he was worried he wouldn't last long enough.)

He wasn't as smooth with women as some guys were, but he knew a woman didn't want to have to compete with a complex algorithm while she was in the throes of passion.

Still, it hadn't seemed to put her off. The way she'd kissed him just before she'd left made him optimistic and, frankly, happy. He hadn't felt simply happy in a long time.

He wanted to call her, and he didn't want to wait—he wanted to hear her voice now. But even with his problematic social skills, he knew better than to do that. He would have to wait at least long enough to convince her he had a modicum of self-control.

He needed to call someone, though, so he called Will.

It was still early, but Will had a young daughter who tended to wake him at the crack of dawn. And this was well past dawn. Surely, Will would be up.

"Chris. How'd it go?" The sound of some cartoon on TV—Chris thought he heard SpongeBob—offered a background to Will's greeting.

"Really well. I wanted to thank you for getting Jackson to send me the recipes. Martina liked the food. The mushroom caps especially."

"No problem. But I can't believe you actually cooked." Will chuckled. "It's like Thurston Howell the Third making his own coconut cream pie—it just doesn't happen."

"Well, it happened this time." Chris was unperturbed by Will's Thurston Howell comparison. "And it was very good ... um ... pie. Metaphorically."

Will hesitated. "If somebody ate somebody else's pie, I don't know if I—"

"We kissed. That's all. Then she thanked me for dinner and went home. It was nice. It was better than nice." Chris found himself grinning like an idiot, and he thought it was probably better Will wasn't here to witness it. Though Will could probably hear the grin over the phone.

"Nice is good," Will said. "Better than nice is very good."

"Yes." After a moment, Chris added, "Though, I'm wondering if maybe I shouldn't have told her about how I got the idea for Play-

Date." Will had heard the story before, and surely he would understand the full implication of what Chris was saying.

"You told her that story?"

"I did."

"But you didn't tell her the entire circumstance, the whole when and where and—"

"Actually, I did." Will's reaction—that surely Chris hadn't been fool enough to do such a thing—made him wonder if it really hadn't been such a good idea.

"Oh. Wow."

Will was too kind to say the word *asshole,* but it was clear he was thinking it.

"This could get to be an issue if Martina and I take things to the next level," Chris admitted.

"You think?"

Well, there was only one thing to do. Chris would have to make sure when the time came, Martina was entirely too busy, and too immersed in pleasure, to have any thoughts at all.

He looked forward to meeting the challenge.

"Fun fact," Martina said at breakfast the morning after her date. "Did you know Chris came up with the idea for PlayDate during sex?"

She, Sofia, and Benny were at the kitchen table with their various breakfast items: Pop-Tarts for Benny, cold cereal for Sofia, and homemade granola with Greek yogurt for Martina.

Benny had been raising a Pop-Tart to her mouth, and the toaster pastry froze in midair. "Wait. What?"

"Not only that," Martina continued, trying to sound casual. "It was while he was losing his virginity."

Sofia let out a rude laugh. "Oh, my God. That's ..."

"I know," Martina said.

She was probably violating Chris's privacy by saying anything to anyone else about it, but she told her sisters everything. Besides, it wasn't as though either of them would ever tell Chris they knew.

"I can't imagine why he told you that," Sofia said. "Usually a guy is so worried about whether you'll think he's a good lover that he edits those kinds of stories. My God, I would."

"But it's kind of cute, right? That he told me, I mean." Martina considered it. "It's cute he wasn't worried about how he'd look or what I'd think, he just told me a true thing. He made himself vulnerable."

Benny rolled her eyes. "There's that word."

"What word?" Martina said.

"*Vulnerable.* Usually you only hear it from therapists and self-help books. And women talking about their crap relationships."

Martina had to conceded the point, except she wasn't talking about a crap relationship—she was talking about a potentially promising one.

"Well, anyway," she went on, "it's sweet, right? Kind of?"

"Yeah," Sofia said, "unless he's thinking about his taxes while he's in bed with you."

"On the other hand," Benny said thoughtfully, "if he's thinking about his taxes, it might give him a little extra endurance, if you know what I mean."

"Unless he's turned on sexually by his taxes," Sofia added. "Which, with a guy like him, is not entirely out of the question."

"So, when are you going to see him again?" Benny asked.

"I don't know. We didn't say."

She was going to have to see him again for his kitchen remodel, obviously. But she wanted to see him sooner than that, and more often. That worried her a little. She liked her independence, and in her experience, when you started to feel like you wanted to see someone soon and often, independence was the first thing to go.

20

O ver the next week, Martina worked on the final designs for Chris's kitchen, firmed up plans for Sofia's wedding shower, and went out with Chris two more times.

On the first of the two dates, they had lunch on the patio at Linn's Easy as Pie Café. On the second, they took a walk on the boardwalk at Moonstone Beach, then had coffee at Jitters on Main Street.

On that second date—the coffee and beach walk date—she mentioned she was going through the process of having Bianca and TJ buy her share of the cabin on Happy Hill. Bianca and TJ had said yes, and she expected to sign the paperwork in the next few days. Bianca and her husband each would have to liquidate some investments to get the money, but it looked like the thing was going to go through.

"Why are you selling them your part of the house?" Chris had asked over lattes and scones. "Are you having money problems?"

"No, no." She shook her head and wiped a bit of milk foam from her upper lip. "It's not that. It's just ... I'm looking to make an investment myself, and I needed the capital."

"Oh. I know something about investments. What is it? Maybe I can help."

But Martina didn't want to tell him, because she wanted this thing to belong to her alone. The fact that he was so wealthy—and the fact that his previous girlfriends had been interested in him mainly for his money—made Martina careful about what she said to him regarding anything financial. She didn't want to seem as though she were angling for his help. And she didn't want that help, in any case. Part of the appeal of the Hall property was that it would be her own thing, her own project from start to finish. Telling him about it seemed like it could go wrong in more than one way.

So she'd put him off. "Just an investment." She toyed with the crumbs from a scone. "I don't even know if it's going to work out, so ..."

She'd left it at that, hoping he wouldn't press for details.

HE DIDN'T PUSH her for more at the time, but now, at home alone, with no one to tell him what might be considered line-crossing, he decided to look into it.

Of course Martina's financial life was none of his business. But what if she hadn't been telling the truth about wanting to make an investment? What if she was having money trouble? If so, he could help. He, better than anyone, could come to her aid if she needed it. And why shouldn't he? They were seeing each other now. No, they hadn't slept together yet, and it was true they didn't have any kind of commitment, but he cared about her. Why wouldn't he want to help?

He started by asking around to see who Martina might be doing business with—and, therefore, to whom she might owe money.

In a town as small as Cambria, it was easy enough to get information about somebody who lived there. Gossip flew, and everyone knew everyone else's business.

It was a little harder for Chris, being a relative newcomer. But that didn't mean it was impossible. He chatted with people at the grocery store and at the post office. He dropped Martina's name during a visit to the gem and mineral show at the Veteran's Hall. He stepped into the historical museum on Burton Drive and mentioned that Martina was working on his kitchen renovation. Had anyone there worked with her on their own homes?

At first, he didn't come up with anything. Then, finally, he spoke to a Realtor who'd sold a home to someone who had hired Martina to get the tired old cottage into shape.

Chris had run into the Realtor at Cambria Coffee as they both sipped from their to-go cups on the patio on a cool weekday morning.

"Do you know her well, then?" Chris had asked, trying to keep his manner casual.

"No, not really. But you know who you should talk to? Riley Whittaker. She's a Realtor in my office. She met with Martina a couple of weeks ago about some property that's on the MLS."

Now they were getting somewhere.

Chris contacted Riley Whittaker, who, to her credit, was a little cagey about it when Chris started to feel her out on her business with Martina.

But Chris got past that by dangling the prospect of a big payday in front of the Realtor.

"Martina's a friend," he told her. "She told me about the property you showed her. I might be interested in buying some investment property myself, and she said I should give you a call."

Riley Whittaker had lit up as though some perfect combination of levers and buttons had been pushed.

"Oh, that's marvelous," she'd said. "Just marvelous. I have some wonderful properties I can show you."

He'd had to tour three of them before getting Riley to spill the information he was after.

"When you see Martina, tell her if she's looking for an investment, she can do much better than the Maxwell Hall property. I mean, yes, it's a good location and the history is intriguing, but it's going to take so much money to rehab it, I hardly think it's worth it."

It had taken two minutes with Google to learn exactly what, and where, the Maxwell Hall property was.

If Chris had been more self-aware, he might have seen that what he'd done was a violation of Martina's privacy. And he was exactly self-aware enough that the thought did occur to him.

But if someone you cared about needed help with something and was too proud to ask for it, was it wrong to do what had to be done to help her anyway? Later, when she found out what he was up to, wouldn't the outcome mean more to her than how it was achieved?

∾

"I NEED you guys to get out of here on Saturday night," Martina told her sisters. "I want to invite Chris over." It was only Thursday afternoon—surely that would give them enough time to make plans.

"You're going to have sex," Sofia said.

Patrick had just come home from the college and was making himself a glass of iced tea in the kitchen. "Ah ... that's too much information," he said.

"I never said I'm having sex. I didn't say sex."

"But that's what you're thinking," Benny said.

"Nooo." Martina was aware the way she'd drawn out the word made it sound as though she were lying. And she wasn't lying—not exactly. She definitely wasn't planning to have sex with Chris, but would there be any harm in letting the batter get to second or even third base? Martina liked second base. Even if they just lingered on first for a while, that could be fun. It all depended on the skill of the shortstop and the power of the bat....

"She's going to have sex," Benny said to Sofia.

Patrick picked up his glass of iced tea and headed toward his room, muttering, "Really, really too much information."

"Okay," Sofia said. "We can think of somewhere to go. Do you need us to be out all night?"

All night seemed a little extreme, given that she didn't know whether the game would go into extra innings. Plus, what if it did? Chris was an adult, and so was she. He could do the walk of shame out the front door in the morning. It wouldn't be unprecedented.

"No," she told Sofia—this time just a regular no, not an elongated one. "Just stay out late, that's all."

"Why don't you go to his place?" Benny was rooting around in the refrigerator for a can of soda. "What's he got over there, ten thousand square feet? Ooh! I heard he's got an observatory. You could do it next to the big telescope." She grinned in a way that suggested the telescope reference was a double entendre.

"He does have an observatory, yes," Martina said. "And I want to invite him here because he's never been here before, and it's a step."

Benny propped a hand on her hip. "Yeah, it is. I get that. Okay. I'll go to a late movie or something."

"Thank you. All of you, I mean it. Thanks."

"You're taking a step," Sofia said. "That's really great. Good for you, Martina."

Benny scowled. "I wish I could take a step with someone. While you're here getting action, I'm going to be getting intimate with a giant tub of buttered popcorn." Benny considered that. "Actually, I've had worse relationships."

21

M artina invited Chris over for dinner, and he showed up looking handsome in a dark sweater and a pair of jeans that perfectly fit his ass. Martina had never had a pair of jeans that fit her ass quite that well, and she mused that it was probably the difference between the three hundred dollar pair Chris was wearing and the Levi's she usually wore, which she picked up for six bucks at the resale store.

He kissed her when she opened the door—they'd reached the point in their relationship when a hello kiss was normal and expected—and she invited him inside and out of the light rain that had left scattered drops in his hair.

They dispensed with the small talk about his day, hers, and the way the food smelled, and she showed him around the house. This part was important, whether he realized it or not. This was her parents' house. It was as close as he would ever come to meeting them.

"The house used to be a brothel," she told him as she led him through the living room and kitchen, the laundry room and the remodeled bathrooms. "See this part here? This is the new construction, where two of the original log cabins were joined together. Each one was only about a thousand square feet, but with the two of them together, plus the addition, it's about twenty-eight hundred—enough room for my sisters and me."

He looked around with interest. "A thousand square feet? That's smaller than I would have guessed for a brothel."

"Well ... I suppose it was a lot different than what you see in the movies."

The Happy Hill neighborhood where Martina lived had gotten its name from the whorehouses that had dotted the area when Cambria had been a mining town. The miners might have been happy here, but Martina doubted the same could be said for the women who'd lived in these cabins. She thought of them sometimes as she lay in bed at night, wondering about their lives.

That was the thing about old houses. They weren't just structures, just walls and roofs and floors and ceilings. They were stories. They were pieces of people's lives.

"So, your parents remodeled this place?" He peered into a small bathroom that artfully combined the rustic feel of the original cabin with modern luxury and convenience. "I'm impressed."

"They didn't do the labor themselves, of course, but the design was all theirs," she told him. "It took them years to get it the way they wanted it. But in the end, it was just right. Every doorknob, every shelf, every piece of furniture was just the way they imagined it."

I am not going to cry, she reminded herself. She'd cried enough in the years following their deaths to fill a swimming pool. She was done crying.

"And you and your sisters inherited it," he said.

Martina recognized that for what it was—an artful way to bring the conversation around to what she'd never talked about with him: her parents' deaths.

"Yes. We did. We discussed whether just one of us should live here—whether one of us should buy out the others. But in the end, none of us wanted to be the one to give it up. Being here, in their place, together—I think it helped all of us get through ... through losing them."

Damn it. I wasn't going to cry. She wiped at her eyes and let out a shaky laugh. If she made light of her emotions, maybe this wouldn't be so awkward.

She finished the tour, took him back to the kitchen, and poured him a glass of wine.

"So," she concluded, "having Bianca and TJ buy my share of the house is a big step for me. But it's time."

For a moment, she thought he wasn't going to ask. And then he did.

"Martina, how did they die?" His voice was soft, as though he could somehow ease the pain of the question or its answer.

Martina lifted the lid from the pot she had simmering on the stove and stirred, using the task as an excuse not to look at him as she talked. "She died of cancer. It was very sudden—she got the diagnosis, and then she was dead a few weeks later, before we could even process what was happening. Then my father had an accident right afterward. He drove his car into a tree."

She didn't have to explain what was obvious: it might not have been an accident. Who could know what Aldo had been thinking in the moments before the impact that had ended his life? Maybe he'd fallen asleep, exhausted by grief.

And maybe he hadn't.

That was too much to contemplate, so she chose not to. She stirred the fragrant contents of the pot, replaced the lid, and changed the subject. They talked about his car project until dinner was ready.

But they both knew what neither of them said: It hadn't only been a step to invite him here, it had also been a step to tell him what she'd just told him. She was letting him into her life. He'd gotten past her emotional gatekeeper.

They both needed to see what he would do now that he was inside the gates.

～

CHRIS DIDN'T TELL Martina what he'd found out about her and the

Maxwell Hall property. If she'd wanted him to know, she'd have told him. He knew he'd crossed a line in poking around for the information on his own, and he knew enough to keep his mouth shut about it.

He'd only been interested in helping her, but she might not see it that way.

Plus, something was happening here that was both precious and fragile: she was letting him in. She'd opened up not only her home but a big part of her emotional life to him, and he didn't want to say anything to make her sorry she'd done it.

Instead, he ate the dinner she'd made—a fragrant Italian stew of tomatoes, onions, garlic, white beans, and vegetables—and simply reveled in her.

Martina wasn't just lovely, though she was that. She wasn't just interesting to talk to, though she was that also. There was some combination of qualities in her—qualities he couldn't quite define— that made her utterly fascinating.

Sitting across from her, he thought he could spend hours observing the way her hair fell against her shoulders or the way she moved, the way her body existed in the world. He found himself thinking about her skin at the oddest times, when he should have been giving his focus to other things. He especially liked the hollow at the base of her throat and that fine bone structure, the way the delicate construction of her wrists made her seem both fragile and miraculous.

Knowing tonight might lead to something more than the few kisses they'd shared made him feel addled, crazy. He did and said the right things, but inside, he marveled that the civilizations of the world had been built and maintained by people who had, at the same time, been driven to distraction by wanting each other. It was amazing anything ever got done.

He was so focused on his need for her he barely noticed that she'd shifted the conversation away from her parents and onto his own.

" ... your mother?"

He only heard the last part of what she'd said. "I'm sorry. You were saying ...?"

"I asked if you're close to your mother." Martina eyed him over the rim of her wineglass.

He smiled, just slightly—a smile that wasn't a smile. "That depends on what you mean by *close*."

Martina tilted her head, looking at him. "Well, tell me what *you* mean by it, and we'll go from there."

His mother. God. There was a topic fraught with difficulty and peril. He'd managed to get through his entire relationship with Alexis without ever acknowledging he had a mother. As far as she'd been concerned, he might have hatched; he might have emerged fully formed from a beam of light.

"My mother is ... problematic." That was understating the issue.

"Oh. I'm sorry. We don't have to talk about it if you don't want to."

To his surprise, he found he did want to. He didn't want to go into the whole shitshow of it—that was for his therapist, if he ever got off his ass and hired one—but he wanted to tell her the basic outline of it. He wanted to get it out there.

"My mother has a drinking problem. A bad one. I try to avoid exposing myself to that as much as possible. I call her regularly to make sure she's okay. I send her money. But ..." The *but* encompassed all of the many things he wished for his relationship with his mother that would never come to pass. An entire world of unfulfilled longing lived in that one word.

"Oh, God. I'm so sorry." Martina gazed at him with sympathy that could also be interpreted as pity. He wanted one, but he didn't want the other. "Did she drink while you were growing up?"

"Yes. She did. That might have been tolerable—something I could navigate—if I'd had a sober parent around to buffer things. But my father left when I was four. I haven't seen him since. I've heard from him, though." He let out a grim laugh. "When PlayDate hit it big and my name started turning up in the news, he called asking for money."

"Oh, no." Martina reached out and put her hand on top of his on the table. "That's awful."

"I gave it to him."

That last bit—how he'd given his father the money he'd asked for —was a constant source of shame. How could he be so desperate for his father's love that he was willing to buy it? But he had been, God help him. He'd been exactly that desperate. It hadn't worked. His father had disappeared again once he'd gotten the money and only got in touch when he needed more.

"It's something we have in common, then," Martina said. "We both lost our parents. It just happened differently for me than it did for you."

She got up from her chair, went to him, and sat in his lap, her arms around his neck. Then she kissed him. She tasted of red wine and some light, flowery perfume.

He was so grateful for the kiss he let himself forget everything else but this.

He didn't need anything else but this.

MARTINA HADN'T KNOWN whether she would sleep with him. Eventually, yes, but she hadn't known whether it would happen tonight. She'd told herself waiting would be wise.

But the next moment, she was taking him by the hand and leading him toward her bedroom.

Was it because he was hurt and she thought she could fix him? Maybe. That's what she did, after all—she took broken things, things that had been neglected, and made them fresh and new again.

She knew better than to try to fix a man. Hadn't her mother told her when she was a teenager—hadn't she told all of them—it was a losing game to try to change someone into the person you wanted them to be?

It had been good advice, no doubt. But right now, she didn't want to think about what was smart and what wasn't. She just wanted to connect with him. They had this thing in common, this awful, painful thing, and if that common bond could lead to something pleasurable, something beautiful, then why shouldn't it?

They went into her room and locked the door in case someone came home earlier than expected. Then she turned to him and pulled the sweater off over his head.

He didn't have the cut physique and six-pack abs of a movie hero. But his body was lean and tanned and somehow vulnerable, as though it had been waiting for her—for some better thing—all this time.

She ran her hands along his skin, and he trembled at her touch.

"Martina, I don't—" He swallowed hard. "I don't want you to do this because of what I said. Because you feel sorry for me. I don't need—"

"*Shh.*" She silenced him with a kiss.

HE TRACED his fingers over that spot that fascinated him—the gentle hollow of her throat. Then he ran his hands gently from her neck to her shoulders, slipping the fabric of her dress off of her skin as he went.

He kissed the spot between her neck and her shoulder, running his tongue along the smooth flesh, and she shuddered.

Chris wanted to be with her now, but he didn't need to. He could wait. He was willing, in fact, to wait as long as it took, as long as either of them needed. More and more, he was sensing that any wait, no matter how long, no matter how difficult, would be worth it.

But here she was, willingly giving herself to him. How could he say no? She was perfection. She was all he'd imagined but had never had.

"Are you sure?" he asked her.

"Just kiss me," she said.

MARTINA HADN'T BEEN with a man in a long time. That was how she'd initially gotten caught up in this, in the idea of Chris. Why shouldn't she have this? Why shouldn't she enjoy some mutually pleasurable lovemaking?

But once she'd touched his skin, once his hands were on her, it became something else. It wasn't just the two of them entertaining each other as consenting adults. Now it was so much more, because she knew she couldn't have shared this moment with just anyone. It could only have been with him.

She stepped out of her dress, which had fallen into a pool of fabric at her feet. Slowly, her eyes on his, she reached down and took off first one shoe and then the other, letting each of them fall to the wood floor with a thump.

She straightened and stepped into his arms. With nothing between them now but a few stray articles of clothing, she felt her body sigh at the meeting of skin on skin. She wanted to melt into him, to disappear into him.

She tipped her head back and he tasted her jaw, letting his mouth trail slowly down.

He unclasped her bra and slid it off her shoulders, then he closed his mouth over the tip of her breast. She let out a ragged gasp at the heat of his tongue on her erect nipple.

She put her hands in his hair and closed her eyes, her head thrown back. Sensations shot through her body—heat, pleasure, electricity.

She wanted more of him, all of him. She unfastened his belt, unsnapping and unzipping his pants and letting them fall. She lay her hand on his hardness through his briefs, and he drew in a sharp breath.

"Lie down," he told her, his voice ragged.

She lay on the bed and waited for him. He stripped the rest of the way and she took in the sight of him, hard and ready for her.

He lay on the bed beside her, and she turned on her side to face him. She wrapped her hand around his length and stroked him, and he moaned in pleasure as she kissed him, caressing his mouth with her tongue.

Her body hummed with sensations. She wanted him touching her, inside her. She lay one leg on his thigh and slid it upward to give him access to her hot, wet core.

He slid his hand inside the waistband of her panties and then lower, finding the slick, soft place that throbbed with need for him. He pushed his fingers inside her, and she quivered with pleasure.

He rolled onto his back, and Martina wiggled out of her panties and straddled him as his hard length pressed against her. She aligned their bodies and lowered herself onto him, taking him in, feeling him fill her.

CHRIS WANTED her so much he wasn't sure how long he was going to last. He didn't want to think of apps or code or his taxes, though. He only wanted to think of Martina—her smell, her skin, the feel of her body wrapped around his. He gripped her hips and moved her on top of him, feeling the inside of her body caressing him.

Right now, with her hair wild and her face the picture of bliss, she'd never been more beautiful. He wasn't sure anyone ever had. He ran his hands up her body and she trembled beneath his fingers.

He wasn't going to hold out long like this, not with her looking into his eyes with such tenderness. So he rolled her onto her back and pulled out of her, with regret, for a moment that felt like forever. He maneuvered her onto her belly and she raised her hips to him. He knelt behind her and found her center, sliding into her with a groan of bliss.

Chris bent over her and pressed his face to her back, tasting her, feeling her heartbeat, as he picked up his rhythm. He reached around and pressed his fingers to the nub where their bodies met, caressing her in time with their movements.

"Oh." She let out a sound that was part word, part animal moan.

"Oh. Oh oh oh. Oh, God ..." Then her body spasmed and shuddered beneath him.

Her pleasure sent him over the edge, and his own release blasted through him in one blinding, devastating surge.

Afterward, they both collapsed onto the bed in a warm, sated jumble. He pulled her into his arms and breathed her in; the feel of her arms around him, the smell of her hair.

He wanted to say something—to thank her, perhaps. But how could he ever adequately thank her for such a thing? Instead, he pulled her closer and kissed her hair.

Chris knew he was in trouble. He knew whatever came after this, he was at her mercy. But even if she chose to wreck him, even if she chose to devastate him and burn his life to black, smoking cinders, he'd have been hard pressed to do anything differently.

So this was how it felt to surrender.

THERE WAS STILL the question of whether Chris should spend the night. If Martina had lived alone, there would have been no issue—of course he would. Of course he'd love nothing better than to wrap her in his arms and drift off to sleep in a bliss of postcoital togetherness.

But she didn't live alone, which made things trickier.

"Do you want me to go?" he asked.

"No." She gave him a slow, languorous grin that undid him. "I want you to stay. But ..."

"But?"

"But then you're going to have to do the walk of shame in the morning. And you'll have to deal with my sisters."

He kissed the tip of her nose. "One man's walk of shame is another man's walk of glory. And I'd love to get to know your sisters."

"Be careful what you wish for," she said.

22

H e woke in the morning feeling better than he had in a long time. Martina was curled up against him, her glorious hair spread over the pillow, her face impossibly lovely in sleep.

Seeing her and feeling her this close to him gave him a hard-on, and his first instinct was to wake her up to recreate the magic of the night before.

But she looked so peaceful he couldn't bear to disturb her. Plus, he needed coffee, and he could already smell it—somebody had gotten up early and made some.

He could admit facing the sisters made him a little nervous. But he'd have to do it sooner or later. And it was worth it for a good shot of caffeine.

Chris slid out of the bed, trying not to wake Martina, and grabbed his clothes off the floor. He dressed and made himself presentable in the little en suite bathroom, then braced himself and went out to face Sofia and Benny.

Neither Sofia nor Benny was out there, though. Instead, he found a studious-looking blond guy huddled over a pile of books and a laptop at the kitchen table.

"Hello." The guy looked up from what he was doing when Chris came in. "You must be Chris." He stood and offered his hand. "I'm Patrick Connelly. Sofia's fiancé."

"Right." Chris shook the hand that had been offered and considered himself lucky he'd avoided the sister gauntlet—at least, for now. "May I?" He gestured toward the coffee pot on the kitchen counter.

"Help yourself. Mugs are in the cupboard over the sink."

Chris got a mug out of the cupboard, poured himself a cup of coffee, and doctored it a bit with some milk and the sugar he found in a bowl on the counter. He was feeling pleased with himself for having avoided the scrutiny of the various Russos in residence when he noticed Patrick was eyeing him.

"So ... getting married, huh?" Chris asked companionably.

"Yes. It's coming up soon."

"You nervous?" Chris leaned his butt against the counter and sipped from his mug.

"No. Actually, I can't wait."

"That's great, man. Congratulations."

"Thank you."

They'd broken the ice somewhat, but Chris could still feel a certain tension in the air, a sense that Patrick wanted to say something he didn't quite have the nerve to say.

"Okay, what?" Chris kept his voice neutral and friendly.

"What do you mean?"

"I get the feeling you want to say something. So, go ahead." Chris gestured with his free arm, a *bring it on* wave of the hand.

"Well ... all right." Patrick shifted in his chair to face Chris more fully. "It's just ... I'm going to be their family pretty soon. I'm going to be Martina's brother-in-law."

"Right. And ..."

"And I care about her, that's all."

"So do I."

Patrick seemed to consider that, and he nodded. "Good. That's good. I just—"

"I don't intend to hurt her, if that's what you're worried about."

"It is." Patrick fidgeted, picking up a pencil from the table and putting it down again. "I know it's none of my business."

"You're right. It's none of your business," Chris said. "But it's kind of nice anyway, knowing people are looking out for her."

Patrick nodded, then turned his focus back to his laptop.

All in all, Chris figured the walk of shame could have gone worse.

It wasn't until later in the day, when Chris had gone home and the women had all returned from their various errands and activities, that Martina had to face interrogation from her sisters.

"Patrick says Chris spent the night." Sofia grinned suggestively. Martina was curled up on the sofa with a book in a patch of late morning sunlight, and Sofia had just come in from a run.

"He told you that, did he?" Martina asked mildly. Of course Patrick would have told Sofia. She'd have expected no less.

"He did. He also said Chris looked smug as hell, so I guess your night went well." Sofia plopped down next to Martina on the sofa. Her spandex running clothes were damp with sweat.

Martina nudged Sofia with her foot. "You're sweaty. Get off the couch until you've showered."

"You're changing the subject," Sofia said.

"I noticed that."

"All right. I'll go. But when I come back, you have to spill."

Benny came in while Sofia was in the shower. She dropped her bag onto the floor near the front door and wasted no time getting to the point. "So, did you get laid last night or not?"

Martina looked up from her book and smiled impassively.

"I can't tell if that's a yes or a go to hell," Benny said, considering the meaning of the smile.

"Can we wait? Sofia's in the shower, and I don't want to have to tell it twice."

"That's fair." Benny went to the refrigerator, pulled out a bottle of Coke, and screwed off the top. "Is it a good story, though? Because I've been looking at plankton under a microscope all morning, and I could really use a good story."

"Wait for Sofia," Martina said.

They didn't have to wait long. A couple of minutes later, Sofia came rushing out of her room dressed in sweatpants and a T-shirt, her hair still wet from the shower.

"Okay! We're all here. What happened? Was he good? Was it fun? Did he rock your world?"

"We're not all here. Bianca's not here," Martina said.

"You're stalling," Benny said. "There's nothing in the rule book that says nonresident Russos have to be present before dissection of someone's sexual experiences."

"There's a rule book?" Sofia asked. "When did that happen?"

Martina was pretending to be reticent because gloating about incredible sex seemed somewhat indecorous. But of course she was going to tell them everything. They were her sisters. Why wouldn't she?

"All right." She put her book down, got up from the sofa, and went into the kitchen where her sisters were standing. She leaned against the countertop and let her giddy joy show. "It was amazing. He was amazing. I don't know if it's because I hadn't had sex in a long time or if it's him ... or me ... but, God."

"Oh, boy." Benny rubbed her hands together in glee. "And he stayed the night?"

"He did," Sofia confirmed. "Patrick saw him early this morning after I left. They had coffee."

"Staying the night is big," Benny said. "I mean, if you're just fooling around, just having fun, you don't stay over. You sneak out in the dead of night with your underwear on backward." She looked at her sisters. "Or, maybe that's just me."

"It's big," Sofia agreed.

"It's not necessarily significant," Martina said. "It's too early to say what is and is not significant."

But privately, she knew they were right. He'd stayed over, and she'd wanted him to. That meant something. Her head knew it was far too early to come to any conclusions about where she and Chris might be headed, but her heart and her body knew what they knew.

"I really like him." Saying it out loud felt scary. She felt vulnerable in a way that was both terrifying and exhilarating.

"Oh, Martina. That's great. You deserve to be happy." Sofia reached out and rubbed Martina's arm.

"You do," Benny agreed, perhaps a bit grudgingly. "Though, if one of us was going to have great sex, I'd have hoped it would be me."

"It will be," Martina said. "You just need to get out there."

"I'm out there every day." Benny's shoulders slumped. "I'm tired of being out there."

So was Martina. The idea that she wouldn't have to be *out there* anymore and could perhaps be tucked safely inside with someone was alluring.

Being *out there* kind of sucked in comparison.

23

Over the next couple of weeks, Martina and Chris saw a lot of each other. She spent the night at Cooper House or he spent the night at the Russo place. Benny and Sofia were getting used to seeing him in their kitchen in the morning and had stopped grilling Martina about the relationship.

The work on Chris's kitchen had moved into the next phase, with demolition scheduled for the following week.

Martina felt a little bit weird about working for Chris, given their budding relationship, but he'd insisted the remodel go forward, and Martina was trying not to dwell on all the ways that could go wrong.

And maybe it wouldn't go wrong. Maybe things would go right. That was always possible, wasn't it?

By the time Chris scheduled a trip to the Bay Area to check on his condo there, meet with his accountant, and deal with various pieces of business, Martina was surprised to realize how entwined in her life he'd become.

"Come with me," he'd said as they were lying in bed at Cooper House one morning, delaying getting up to start their day. They'd just had satisfying, languorous sex, and she was tucked up against his body, her arms around him.

"I can't. I have work. I've got projects underway, and I can't leave."

"You're your own boss," he reminded her. "Who's going to tell you that you can't take a few days?"

"Me. I'm the one who's telling me that." She pushed back from him a little to look at him more fully. "I'm working like hell to build my business, and I can't do that if I blow off my clients. I've got schedules to stick to and people who are relying on me. Noah's crew—"

"Okay." He kissed her. "I get it. That's fine. I'll be back in a few days."

She settled in against him, her head against his chest so she could hear his heartbeat.

"Only ..."

"Only what?" She raised up to look at him again.

"I'm just saying, it's not like you have to worry about your income."

Her eyes widened in surprise. "Why don't I have to worry about my income?"

"Cooper House is a big job, that's all. A big, expensive job. So if you have to put off your other clients ..."

Martina didn't like where this was going, and a hard knot of dread settled in her stomach. She got up from the bed and pulled a throw blanket around her to cover her body.

"What are you saying? That you're giving me work at Cooper House so I can ... what? So I can be free to take trips with you?"

He rose onto his elbow, his head propped on one hand. "I didn't say that."

"But it sounded like that's what you meant."

"Well, I didn't. I just meant your business is doing well right now, and maybe you could take a few days and relax a little bit. That's all." He patted the space on the bed where she'd been. "Lie back down. Please?"

The whole thing—the link between his wealth and the health of her business—unsettled her. It had always been her suspicion that Alexis had been with Chris for his money, and who knew how many other women that had been true for? She didn't want to be one of them, and she didn't want him to think, even for a moment, that she was.

"I don't want your business because of our relationship." She stubbornly stood her ground instead of letting herself be lured back into bed before this was settled.

"I know. And that's not why you have it. You got the job before we started seeing each other."

"Yes, but—"

"The kitchen looks like it belongs in a Holiday Inn. It needs you."

That was true. It did, on both counts.

When she still didn't move toward him, he said, "If it helps, I promise not to give you any more work once the kitchen is done. I'll find someone else to do the rest of the house. Or I'll just leave it as is. It's not worth it if it's going to be an issue for you."

"Well ..."

"Well what?"

She grinned—she couldn't seem to help it—and dropped the throw blanket she'd been using to cover herself. She lay back down and snuggled up to his warm body. "I don't want you to replace me."

She said it as though she meant she didn't want him finding a new designer. And she didn't. But she didn't want to be replaced here, in bed, either. That was something she worried about more than she wanted to admit. Because before Alexis, there had been others. And those others had been so much more polished, so much more smooth and rich and sophisticated than Martina.

All of this—the relationship, the Cooper House job, Chris's money—made her feel like she was trying on a life that didn't quite fit her, like she was playing dress-up in her mother's closet.

Maybe I can make it fit, she thought. *A nip here, a tuck there ...*

She didn't delve too deeply into the implications of that.

∽

CHRIS DIDN'T WANT to go to the Bay Area without Martina. But the moment his comment about not worrying about her income had come out of his mouth, he knew he'd made a critical error.

Because the fact was, he *had* meant it the way she'd thought he did. He *had* meant he would ensure her income so she could go out of town with him, or stay in bed all day, or ... whatever they wanted, really. What was the point of having all this money if he couldn't use it to give both of them what they wanted?

And what he wanted right now was to spend time with Martina.

But she wasn't like the other women in his life, women who considered it their birthright to be taken care of financially. If he treated her like she was one of them, she was going to pull back—just the way she had that morning.

So, once she'd left for work, he packed a bag for his trip to the Bay Area and resolved to be okay with going alone. It was probably good, actually.

He was falling into this thing with her so quickly, so completely, it would be healthy to have a little time to himself.

That's what he told himself, anyway.

MARTINA HAD BOOKED the venue for Sofia's bridal shower—they'd be doing it in a private room at Neptune—but she still had to work on details like decorations and entertainment. Neptune didn't offer special event cakes, so Martina had ordered one from a local bakery.

She was also working out the last details of getting her deposit and down payment ready to make an offer on the Hall property. Martina had applied for mortgage preapproval, and that was still in process. She thought she would probably be approved—her credit score was excellent—but who knew? Owning her own business meant she didn't have a guaranteed steady income. Money came and went. Her income over the past couple of years looked healthy, but there was no telling whether the lender would think it was enough.

Noah was finishing a bathroom remodel for Martina, so she had to give her attention to that as well. She visited the work site, kept the client updated on progress, and prepared to do the final touches like selecting window treatments and paint color.

She had a lot to think about, and that was good, because it distracted her from what Chris had said during that conversation in his bedroom.

Had he really been suggesting he would support her so she could go running off to the Bay Area with him? Had he really meant now that they were together, she no longer had to tend to her job—her career—the way she otherwise would?

So much about that bothered her. She tried not to think about it at Lowe's as she picked out towel bars and soap dishes for her client's bathroom. But the more she tried to push it out of her mind, the more it resurfaced.

It's just a misunderstanding. In any relationship, there are going to be misunderstandings.

Hopefully, she had set him straight on it, and there wouldn't be another problem. But what if she hadn't? What if he didn't get it?

Her cell phone rang while she stood in the bathroom fixtures aisle, pondering the pros and cons of a particular style of towel rod.

Benny.

"Hey, Martina. Can you pick up toilet paper while you're out? We ran out, and I'm on the way to work, and Sofia's going to be at the office late, so ..."

"Sure. I can get some." Martina was distracted, and she must have sounded that way.

"What's wrong?"

"What? Nothing. Why?"

"Oh. I know what it is." Martina could hear road noise in the background as Benny drove. "You miss your big, sexy, multimillion-aire man toy."

She did, but she didn't want to admit it.

"I do not."

"Do too. He went up north without you, and you're wondering

what he's doing up there, surrounded by all those glossy society women."

"What makes you think he's surrounded by glossy society women?"

In fact, he probably was. The Alexises of the world gravitated toward men like Chris—men with more money then sense about interpersonal relationships.

"Oh, just the fact that glossy society women love rich guys the way high school girls love Sephora. It's a thing."

"Is it? Do you know everything about it? Why don't you just call him, then, and suggest he go back to Alexis?" It had come out angrier and harsher than Martina had intended. Maybe she wasn't as good at managing her insecurity as she seemed.

"Hey, now. I was just kidding." Benny sounded concerned, and that wasn't what Martina wanted.

"I know. I'm fine. Everything's fine."

"Oh, boy. One *fine* is convincing. Two is an outright lie."

Martina put down the towel holder she was carrying and focused on the phone call, trying to keep her voice low so the man shopping for shower curtains halfway down the aisle from her wouldn't hear. "He asked me to go with him, but I said no."

"Okay ..."

"Because I had work! I have clients! I have things to do! And ..."

"And what?"

"And, he suggested maybe, now that I'm with him, I don't have to worry about little, petty considerations like work anymore."

Benny was silent for a moment. Then: "Holy shit."

"Right."

"What's he getting at? He's not planning to propose, is he? You guys have been together about five minutes."

"No, not that. At least, I really don't think so."

"Then, what? He's planning to make you his kept woman? Set you up in a style to which you'll soon become accustomed so you can be available at his beck and call?"

Now Martina was the one who was silent.

"Holy shit," Benny said again.

"That's what I'm worried about," Martina said. "Because I'm not doing that. That isn't who I am."

"I know it's not. And if he's not an idiot, he does, too."

24

Chris was still at his Silicon Valley condo when Riley Whittaker called him. At first, he couldn't remember exactly who she was. When she started trying to sell him real estate, it all became clear.

"I was just wondering if you had any thoughts on those properties I showed you," she said. "If none of those appeal to you, I have a couple of new listings that might be just right for you."

He closed his eyes. Ah, yes. The Realtor. The one he'd visited when he'd wanted to pump her for information about Martina.

"I'm not in town right now," he told her. "Maybe give me a call when I'm back in Cambria." He didn't really need to hear from her—he wasn't in the market for property—but if Martina was still trying to buy that house on Lodge Hill, it might be wise to stay in touch.

"Oh, of course. And when will you return?"

They chatted about that for a moment, and then, making small talk, Chris asked, "So, how is business going for you?"

There was nothing a Realtor loved more than talking about which properties had and had not sold, and for how much. She launched into a discussion of which neighborhoods were hot, which were not, and the trends in property values.

He was getting ready to wrap up the phone call when she said, "And, surprisingly, I've gotten an offer on that Maxwell Hall property we talked about—the one Martina was interested in."

"Really." The way she'd said it, it was clear Martina was not the one who'd made the offer.

"Yes! I couldn't believe it. But, the offer was from someone who wants to raze the house and use the existing water meter to build new construction, so that makes sense. It's a lovely location."

"It really is," he said.

She was still happily chatting about it when he excused himself, saying he had a meeting he was late for. There was no meeting—he'd already seen his accountant, and he had nothing else scheduled for the day—but Riley had shown no signs of slowing down, so he'd had to extricate himself.

After he hung up, he considered the implications of the phone call, and he began to form a plan.

A good plan.

He actually whistled as he continued his day.

MARTINA GOT her loan approval on a Thursday morning, the day Chris was scheduled to come back from the Bay Area.

"I got it!" she yelled to the house at large before realizing everyone had already left for work and she was talking to no one. Impulsively, she jumped up from her seat on the sofa, where she'd been looking at her laptop, and did a little victory dance, shaking her hips and waving her fists in the air.

She knew it was a bad idea for a buyer to deal directly with a seller's agent, so she'd arranged days before to work with Joe Barkley, an agent she knew from her design work.

She called Joe and got him on the first ring.

"I want to make an offer," she said before she'd even greeted him.

"Martina?"

"I got the loan approval. I want to put in an offer on the Hall property."

"Oh. That's great." She heard him tapping on his keyboard. Then she heard an ominous silence.

"Joe?"

"It's in escrow." He sounded both apologetic and dismayed. "Shit. It was still listed as available last night, but this morning ... I've got it on the MLS as sale pending."

"No!" Martina exclaimed. "How can that be? Who would even want it? Have they seen the house? It's falling down!"

"Somebody did want it. Martina, I'm sorry. I told the seller you'd be making an offer soon, but I guess somebody else got in there first."

"But I have the loan approval!"

"I didn't expect this," Joe said. "But, look. There's no guarantee it'll make it through escrow. A sale like this, with a damaged structure ... You might still have a chance."

She got off the phone feeling crestfallen. All of this effort, all of this work—the loan documents, everything she'd gone through to get the down payment, everything Bianca and TJ had done to get her the money. Now, not only wasn't she going to get the property, she no longer owned a part of her parents' home. She had nothing but a pile of money and a worthless piece of paper from a mortgage company.

She called Riley Whittaker before her outrage had dissipated.

"Who bought the Hall property?" she demanded to know.

"It's confidential," Riley said.

"Confidential, my ass."

"Really, it's an anonymous buyer. Even if I wanted to tell you, I don't know."

"Well ... shit."

"If you're still interested in investing in some property, I have other homes I can show you. Even one on Lodge Hill that—"

Martina hung up while she was still talking.

～

"JEEZ, THAT REALLY DOES SUCK," Benny told her that afternoon, when the two of them were at Jitters drinking lattes amid the afternoon tourist crowd. "You put a lot into getting ready to make an offer."

"I really did." Martina looked glumly into her latte mug. Tears sprang to her eyes and she blinked hard to clear them. "I really wanted this, Benny. I wanted to restore it, to bring it back to what that house should be. And the land ... I wanted to keep it just the way it is. It's so beautiful! Whoever bought it is going to bulldoze the trees and the house and put up, what? A five-bedroom stucco monstrosity with a hot tub?"

"Probably," Benny admitted.

"Well, that's just *bullshit*," Martina grumbled.

"I'm sorry it didn't work out."

"Me too."

Martina had known buying the property meant a lot to her, but she hadn't realized exactly how much until she knew it wasn't going to happen. The letdown was excruciating.

She'd built an entire fantasy life for herself around the property. She'd imagined herself living in the restored house amid the trees and the wildflowers, deer grazing just outside her door, the interior of her home designed with her own aesthetic in mind, giving an artistic and tasteful nod to the house's mid-century modern history.

And, she had to admit, she'd imagined more, too. She'd imagined living there with Chris and their eventual children. It had been a beautiful dream.

And now what did she have? The dream wasn't going to happen. The house wasn't going to be hers—and now, the house she lived in didn't belong to her, either. Of course, she knew she could stay there as long as she needed to; she and Bianca had worked out a rental agreement. But that wasn't the same as having something of her own.

On top of that, she hadn't realized how much she was going to miss Chris until he was actually gone, up there in the Bay Area with his rich friends doing God knew what.

She didn't really suspect he was doing anything that would upset her. If he'd planned to be with another woman, for instance, he never would have invited Martina to go with him.

Still, that part of his life was another world to her, one she knew nothing about.

Also, there was the emptiness in her bed with him gone. It shocked her how quickly she'd gotten used to waking up with him beside her. Her reality had shifted so fast she was left breathless. A gnawing ache in her chest pulled at her when he wasn't around, and she didn't like it. How was she supposed to get on with her life when every part of her hurt?

She didn't mind wanting him—that was fine. But the needing was another thing. She didn't know how she felt about needing someone this way.

CHRIS DECIDED to come home via Highway 1 and Big Sur. He'd taken the S 65—a convertible Mercedes that was worth more than the house he'd grown up in—and the day was unseasonably warm for January. So he put the top down for the drive south on the winding, two-lane road. Pine-covered peaks towered above him to his left, and the rocky, crashing surfline frothed far below him to his right.

He told himself to enjoy the drive instead of rushing to get home to Martina. Hell, that was why he'd decided to take the scenic route instead of the quicker, more direct inland route. It was an attempt to convince himself he could have a good time without Martina with him. Because he was beginning to doubt it, and that was a worrisome development.

He'd taken his time during this trip, tending to things at his condo, having dinner with friends, and doing all of the things he would usually do if he didn't have someone waiting for him in Cambria.

But instead of enjoying all of it, he found himself counting the days and hours until he could go back down the coast and see his girlfriend.

He was pretty sure if he ever decided to see a therapist about his relationship issues—which he knew he should do—he'd be told he needed to be comfortable with himself before he could have a healthy relationship with someone else.

And yet, here he was, itchy inside his own skin, feeling this uncomfortable longing.

A big misconception about wealth was that a person stopped longing once they got enough money to do anything they wanted. He, himself, had harbored that same misconception. The truth was, the longing never went away. There was always something he wanted but couldn't have, and having money didn't change that.

Right now, he wanted Martina.

And, he had something important to tell her—something he thought would make her happy. Making her happy was going to make him happy as well, he was sure of it.

If only he could change this feeling that he still wasn't quite doing things right in his relationship with her. He had this nagging sense he was still making mistakes that might derail the whole thing—he just didn't know what they were.

On the way south, he stopped in Gorda and got a sandwich at a little restaurant overlooking the ocean. He tried to call Martina, but there was no cell service here.

Damn it.

Well, it was more practice being okay, wasn't it? Another opportunity to master the art of spending a day by himself without feeling like he was missing a limb.

It was a damned hard thing to manage.

25

A s much as Martina's day had sucked, at least she was looking forward to seeing Chris that night. He'd texted her when he got back into town, and she was set to meet him at Cooper House as soon as she finished work.

After her last client appointment for the day, she went home, took a shower, shaved her legs, put on her best matching bra and panty set —white silk with lace trim—and selected an outfit.

She wanted to look casual but not too casual, sexy but not too sexy. She wanted to look like she hadn't gone to too much trouble to get ready but nevertheless had emerged all dewy-skinned and perfect from a mystical forest full of unicorns and wood sprites just to make his erotic fantasies come true.

It was a lofty goal, and one she wasn't quite sure she'd met. Still, he seemed glad to see her when she went into Cooper House and found him in the foyer, waiting for her.

He enfolded her in his arms, and her whole body sighed in response.

"It's good to see you," he murmured into her hair.

"You too." Her words were muffled because her face was pressed into his chest. She smelled the clean laundry scent of his shirt and, beneath that, the warm musk of his body. "How was your trip?"

"Fine. Lonely. I'll tell you all about it."

She tipped her face up to him. "Maybe later."

He kissed her, and she thought, *Yes. This.*

"Later's good." He took her by the hand and led her to the bedroom.

AFTER THEY'D MADE love and showered and they were standing, half dressed, in the kitchen looking for something to eat, he told her about what he'd done while he was gone.

He'd had the meeting with his accountant, mostly focused on his income tax return; he'd had dinner with a friend, a guy who'd worked with him to develop PlayDate and who had bought the company when Chris had decided to retire; and he'd gathered some clothes and other things from his condo he'd forgotten to bring the last time he came to Cambria.

"Sounds productive." Martina looked in the refrigerator and selected a carton of yogurt the caretaker at Cooper House had bought during Chris's absence. Martina had been surprised to find the kitchen fully stocked—one of the perks, apparently, of wealth. She didn't envy Chris many of the trappings of money, but it would be great never to have to go grocery shopping again.

"It was productive." He sipped beer from a longneck bottle as he leaned against the counter, watching her. He was shirtless, and his jeans were open at the top button. "How about you? How were things while I was gone?"

Her face fell. She'd tried not to think about the Hall property because she'd wanted to simply enjoy being with Chris. But now that he'd brought it up, the disappointment hit her anew.

"It was okay, mostly. But ..."

"But?"

"But someone bought the property I was interested in. The investment opportunity I told you about? It was a house for sale on Lodge Hill. I went to put an offer on it, and it was already in escrow." Tears sprang to her eyes, and she wiped them away, laughing bitterly at herself. "It's stupid. I'm sorry. I shouldn't be this upset over something that was never mine to begin with."

He was giving her a look that was almost ... pleased.

"What?" she asked.

His mouth curved into a slow half grin. He put down his beer and came to her. "What if I said you can still have the property?"

She froze. "What?"

He gathered her into his arms and rubbed her back through the T-shirt—his—that she was wearing. "I'm the one who bought it. I wanted to surprise you."

At first, she wasn't sure she'd heard him right. "You ... Wait. *What?* How did you even know about it?" She pushed back from him so she could see his face more fully.

"I asked around, and I found out you were looking at the property. Then I heard someone had made an offer on it. I didn't want you to lose it, so I put in a higher bid. It's in escrow. It's yours."

Martina's jaw dropped. She stepped farther away from him and stood with her arms crossed over her chest, her face a mask of outrage. "Chris ... You can't just *do* things like this. What's wrong with you?"

CHRIS WAS BEGINNING to think he'd made an important tactical error, but for the life of him, he didn't know what it was. Why wasn't she happy? Why wasn't she kissing him in gratitude? He'd been certain this would make her see him as a hero. Why didn't she?

"Martina, I thought this would be good news. I thought you'd be glad."

She paced the room, looking so beautiful wearing nothing but his T-shirt, her long legs bare and lean, her hair still mussed from lovemaking, that he could hardly focus on the argument they were about to have.

"I wanted to do this myself. I wanted to buy the property myself."

"But someone had put an offer on it. You were going to lose it. I thought—"

"Explain to me how you knew someone had put an offer on it. Explain how you knew I wanted to buy it in the first place. Why did you 'ask around'?"

He had to tread carefully here. There were a lot of ways this part of the conversation could go wrong. "I talked to Riley Whittaker, and she told me." That seemed safe enough.

"Riley Whittaker." Martina said the name more to herself than to him.

"Yes."

"How do you know Riley Whittaker?"

"She showed me some properties a while back. She called me to ask if I'd thought any more about them, and the subject of the Hall property came up."

"It came up."

She was repeating things, and that seemed like a bad sign.

"Yes."

"So, with all of the properties on the market, all of the things available or in escrow or with offers on them ... she just happened to mention the Hall property to you, and she just happened to tell you I wanted it." She was eyeing him with suspicion, and he felt like he was being interrogated by a particularly canny FBI agent.

"Well ... I'd asked her about it. When she showed me properties, before."

"You asked about it."

"Martina, you keep repeating the things I say. It's unsettling."

"I don't care." She paced some more, and he felt himself starting to sweat. "And why did you ask about it? It doesn't seem like the kind of property you'd be interested in."

He wasn't going to be able to pull off lying about it. That much was clear. He closed his eyes, took a deep breath, and told her the truth.

"When you said you needed money for an investment, I was worried maybe you were going through some financial problems. I thought ... Well, I thought maybe I could help. So I asked around a little. And I found Riley Whittaker, and I ... I maybe led her to believe I already knew your plans."

She gaped at him, her jaw slack, eyes wide. "You spied on me?"

It sounded bad when she said it that way, so he reframed it. "I just asked around."

"What gave you the right to ask people about my personal business?"

God, she was beautiful when she was mad. He tried not to let that distract him. He had to keep his head in the game.

"Martina. I think we're losing sight of the fact that you almost lost the property to another buyer, but now you can have it. That was the goal, wasn't it? You wanted it, and now it's going to be yours."

He'd thought the logic of that might calm her, but it had the opposite effect. She whirled toward him in a rush of righteous fury. "It's going to be mine because *you* bought it," she said. "What's your plan? To give it to me? That property is half a million dollars. Were you just going to hand it over like a bouquet of flowers or a box of chocolates?"

"Of course not." In fact, it was exactly what he'd planned to do, but considering her anger, it seemed imprudent to say so.

She let out a harsh laugh. "Really. You were going to let me set up a payment plan with late payment penalties and a competitive interest rate? Somehow, I don't think that was what you had in mind."

He was losing a fight he hadn't anticipated having. Why were they fighting, when he'd intended to do something nice for her? When he'd meant to make her happy? He rubbed at his face with both hands, suddenly exhausted.

"What if I did plan to give it to you? So what? Is that so wrong?"

She stared at him as though she couldn't believe he'd said it. Then her shoulders fell, and she wouldn't look at him. She walked out of the room, closing the door behind her. In a moment, he heard her walking up the stairs.

He followed her up and found her hurriedly getting dressed.

"What are you doing?" But he knew what she was doing—she was leaving.

"I'm going home."

"Why?"

"*Why*?" There was that look again—the one that said he was such a fool that it defied credibility. "Because I'm not Alexis. Unlike the Hall property, I can't be bought."

She pulled on her sweater, slipped on her shoes, grabbed her things, and left.

As Chris watched her go, his instinct was to go after her. But his instinct didn't seem to work for shit these days, so he didn't do it. Instead, he listened to the distant sound of her car starting up and driving away.

26

Martina started banging things around the moment she got home. She started with the door, which she slammed, then moved on to her purse, which she flung to the floor. She was about to hurl her messenger bag against the wall, when she remembered her computer was in there. Instead, she put it down gently, though it took her some effort to restrain herself.

It was late, and the house was dark. At the sound of Martina's angry noises, her sisters began to open their bedroom doors.

"What's going on out here?" Sofia was squinty-eyed, her hair mussed. She was wearing a pair of plaid flannel pajamas to stay warm in the chilly house.

"Seriously. What the hell?" Benny looked more perky. Apparently she'd been watching TV instead of sleeping, because Martina could hear the tinny sounds of sitcom dialogue coming from inside Benny's room.

"Is everything okay?" Patrick poked his head out into the hallway. "I heard something. Was there a break-in? Do I need to call somebody?"

"It's fine. Everything's fine. Just leave me the hell alone." Martina turned her back on them so they wouldn't see she was near tears.

"Oh, boy. This has something to do with Richie Rich, obviously," Benny said.

"Oh, no." Sofia turned to Patrick. "This is girl stuff. Go back to sleep." She kissed him, and he retreated back into their room.

Sofia and Benny came into the living room. Part of Martina wanted to tell them everything and have them console her, the way sisters did. And another part of her just wanted them to leave her alone because she didn't want to admit she'd been so stupid.

"Come on. Sit down. Tell your favorite sister everything." Benny sat on the sofa and patted the cushion beside her.

"She can't. Bianca's not here," Sofia quipped.

Benny shot Sofia a middle finger, then returned her attention to Martina. "Seriously, Martina. What happened?"

Martina gave in to the part of her that wanted commiseration. What would the point be in hiding what had happened? They'd know eventually. And if she couldn't tell her sisters how big an idiot she'd been, then who could she tell?

"Chris and I had a fight."

"No shit," Benny said. "I gathered that much. About what? What did he do?"

A few tears were falling now, and Martina wiped them away. She sat beside Benny on the sofa while Sofia settled into a chair on the other side of the coffee table.

"He bought the Maxwell Hall property."

Sofia and Benny looked at each other. Then Sofia said, "But ... why? Did he know you wanted it?"

"That's why. That's the reason. He bought it for me. That *asshole*."

"Hold up." Benny put up her hands in a traffic-cop gesture. "Are you saying he bought a piece of property worth more than I'll make in six years ... so he could *give* it to you?"

"That's what I'm saying."

Benny let out a laugh. "Well, I'd have settled for a bouquet of flowers, but that works, too."

"Benny!" Martina was outraged.

"I mean," Benny went on, "if your gazillionaire boyfriend can't buy you a prime piece of property, who can?"

"Stop," Sofia told Benny. "I get it. I do. It's too much, too soon. And she wanted to do it herself. She wanted it to be hers."

"Yes! Exactly! And he took that away from me."

"Okay." Sofia's voice was soothing. "But, back up a little. Why did he do that? How did it come about?"

So Martina told both of them the whole story: how Chris had gone behind her back to learn about her financial affairs; how he'd found out she wanted the Hall property but someone else had made an offer on it; and finally, how he'd bought it himself. She recounted the fight, including the way Chris had admitted he'd intended to give the property to Martina.

"He wasn't even going to let me pay for it! Which makes me, what? A prostitute? A whore? A gold digger?"

"I'm pretty sure you're not a prostitute unless you set the terms in advance," Benny said. "As for the gold digger thing, that implies you're only with him for his money. He surprised you with this, and you didn't even want it, so it doesn't count."

"It's not about whether she actually *is* a gold digger," Sofia clarified for Benny. "It's that now, she *feels* like one."

"Yes!" Martina said. "And obviously he sees me that way, or he wouldn't have done this. He wouldn't have thought he had to."

"Well ... not necessarily." Benny had dropped some of her smartass attitude and seemed to be honestly considering it. "Wealthy people don't think the same as the rest of us do. When he found out the property had an offer on it and you might not get it, he probably thought, why not? That kind of money is nothing to him. If he could make you happy, why not do it?" Martina glared at her, and she put her hands up in surrender. "I'm not saying he was right. I'm just saying, that's probably what he thought."

"So, how did you leave it?" Sofia asked. "What did you tell him about the property?"

"I didn't tell him anything. I got mad, and he insisted he'd meant to sell it to me, and I called bullshit, and he finally admitted he'd meant to just give it to me. So I left. I don't know what's going to happen now. I still want the property, but I can't accept it from him. It just doesn't feel right." She wrung her hands in her lap. "And there are bigger issues! Like, why was he stalking around, asking about my private financial business!"

"That really is creepy," Benny admitted.

"And he thinks he has to buy his women," Sofia added. "Because that's obviously what he was trying to do. I mean, look at how he was with his ex. He was going to remodel Cooper House just because she wanted him to. And their relationship wasn't even that serious!"

Martina slumped into the cushions on the sofa, her head back, looking at the ceiling. Her face felt hot and her middle felt hollowed out. "It's just not right—any of it. I don't want to be bought. I don't want him doing things for me that I want to do for myself. I don't want him thinking I'm only around for the perks. And I don't want to feel that I can't make reasonable decisions regarding the relationship because ... because ..."

"Because you're in hock to him for five hundred grand," Benny supplied.

"Right." Martina let out a ragged breath. "God, this is so messed up."

Sofia moved from her chair to the sofa, sitting down on Martina's other side. She put a hand on Martina's shoulder and squeezed. "So, what are you going to do?"

"Break up with him, I guess."

"Is that what you want?" Sofia asked.

"No." And, damn it, there were more tears. She squeezed her eyes shut and rubbed them with her fingertips. "No, damn it. It's not what I want."

"Then I think you two are going to need to have a come to Jesus talk," Benny said.

∽

CHRIS KNEW he'd made a terrible mistake with Martina. He just didn't know exactly what it was.

He'd listened to her while she was yelling at him, so he did understand some of her complaint. She'd wanted to buy the property herself, for one thing. Okay, he got that. But someone had made an offer. What was he supposed to do, just let the other party buy the house and the land and let Martina be disappointed? Why, when there was something he could easily do to correct the situation?

Then there was the part about her not being for sale. That one was harder for him to comprehend. When, exactly, had he said he wanted to buy her? When had he said he expected anything in return for what he'd done? He'd done something nice, for Christ's sake. Something considerate. Since when did a guy get kicked in the balls —metaphorically speaking—for that?

She'd said the thing about Alexis, too. How she wasn't like Alexis. Well, of course she wasn't. Martina couldn't be any different from Alexis if the two of them had come from different planets. So, why had Alexis's name even come up in the conversation?

All of it was giving him a headache, so he took a couple of Tylenol before going back to bed. Alone.

The Tylenol didn't help—not really—so he got up and got himself a couple of fingers of whiskey from the bar cart in the library. He sat in a chair by the dark, cold fireplace, sipping and thinking.

Was he that dense when it came to women? Was he so entirely clueless that he could get in a huge fight with his girlfriend, get yelled at about what he'd done, and still have no idea whatsoever about how he'd fucked up?

Yes, asshole. You're exactly that clueless.

He wanted to fix this, but how could he when he didn't know where he'd gone wrong?

One thing he absolutely couldn't do was ask Martina to explain it to him. If she realized that not only wasn't he sorry for what he'd done, but that he didn't even know what it was or why she was upset, she was going to dump his ass for sure.

There were many thing he didn't know about women, but one

thing he did know was they didn't like to be misunderstood, and if they *were* misunderstood, they took it as definitive proof the person who'd misunderstood them needed to be cut off—not only from sex, but from their lives.

Finished. Done. Delete their contact information and block them on Twitter.

He didn't want to be that guy. He didn't want to get ghosted.

He rubbed his forehead, feeling like one miserable son of a bitch.

This evening had started so well, too.

He didn't want to sleep alone—not with the memory of Martina so fresh—but it seemed he didn't have a choice. He finished his drink, went upstairs, and got into bed, hoping things would look clearer in the morning.

27

M artina knew she should probably break up with Chris. But, as she'd told her sisters, she didn't want to do that. She wasn't in love with him—it was too soon for that. But she had to admit things were heading that way, and that didn't happen every day. It seemed like a shame to throw that away without even trying to have the come to Jesus talk her sisters had recommended.

But what would she say? How could she get through to him?

She didn't know, so she decided to take a break from him while she thought about it.

He called her cell phone in the morning, but she didn't answer. She didn't want to ignore him, though, so she sent him a text message.

I'm not ready to talk yet. I need a little time.

That seemed much more civilized than simply refusing to take his calls.

His answer came quickly: *But you are willing to talk about it? This isn't over, is it? I hope it's not.*

She hesitated, then typed: *We'll talk. Just not yet.*

First, she had to think about exactly what she wanted to say, how she wanted to say it, and what kind of result she wanted.

Right now, none of those answers was entirely clear.

～

As CHRIS'S most recent ex, Alexis might have had some insight into why he kept screwing things up with women.

He called her one afternoon when he was out in his garage looking at the broken pieces of his Mustang. He'd been trying to work on the car, but he was so distracted by his thoughts about Martina he kept making mistakes that were going to cost him both time and money.

He leaned against his work bench, pulled his phone out of his back pocket, and called her.

At first, she refused to pick up the phone. Of course she was screening his calls. Then, he texted her.

Just pick up, Alexis. I need to talk to you.

He tried again, and this time she answered.

"What do you want?" The hostility in her voice took him aback and made him wonder if maybe he were beyond help when it came to women.

"Look, Alexis. I don't want to fight. I just wanted to ask you something."

"Fine. What is it? I have to be somewhere in ten minutes."

He was sure she'd just said that to put him on the defensive. Well, fine. He'd try to make this quick.

"Am I ... Shit, I don't know how to put this." He rubbed his forehead with his free hand.

"Try. I'm in a hurry."

He let out a breath. "Am I really awful to be in a relationship with? And if so, how? Specifics would be helpful."

She didn't say anything for a moment, and he took her silence for surprise.

"Alexis?"

"Christopher, what the hell is this about?"

"I just ... God. I'm seeing someone, and it's not going well. And I really want it to go well. But I don't know how to fix it if I don't know what I'm doing wrong. So, tell me. What did I do wrong? What's wrong with me?"

Another stretch of silence. Then: "That's going to take a lot longer than ten minutes."

SINCE MARTINA WASN'T willing to see him right now, he had nothing better to do than drive to the Bay Area to see Alexis. She'd agreed to meet him for lunch the following day to dissect his failings.

That was likely to be as much fun as a root canal without anesthesia, but from his perspective, being alone for the rest of his life would be even less fun than that.

He met her at Chez Panisse in Berkeley, and they sat at a quiet table covered with white linen in the back of the restaurant. The dark, warm wood tones of the dining room made him feel as though he'd been transported to somewhere far away from his own life and all of its complications.

But Alexis was here to remind him of them.

"So," he said when they each had a glass of wine in front of them and had placed their lunch orders with the waitress.

"So," she repeated. "You came all the way here so I can tell you what's wrong with you?" She was impeccably dressed in black slacks and a white silk blouse, her hair and makeup perfect. She looked as though she'd just come from being professionally styled.

"Yes. I suppose so. I came all the way here to find out why I keep screwing up with women. You're the most recent woman I've screwed up with, so ..." He left the rest hanging there.

She looked at the table instead of at him. She picked up her wineglass, took a delicate sip, then put it back down precisely in the same place it had been before. Then she focused on him.

"Who is it?"

"Who is what?"

"Who are you seeing, Christopher? You said you were seeing someone, and that's why we're here. Who is it?"

He thought about refusing to tell her, because who would it serve for her to have that information? But then he decided, in the interests of honesty and openness, to come out with it.

"I'm seeing Martina Russo."

Alexis's eyes widened. "The designer?"

"Yeah."

"You didn't waste any time, did you?"

That threw him off a little. "What do you mean?"

"I mean, if our relationship were a dead body, it wouldn't have even been cold when you started seeing her. I'm assuming, given the circumstances. You really can't stand being alone, can you?"

"Oh, come on. That's not fair." But, was it? She was right—he'd started seeing Martina very soon after breaking up with Alexis. But that was just a coincidence. When you met someone who was right for you, you had to act, didn't you?

Or was it because he couldn't stand to be alone?

She fixed him with a look that penetrated him. "You asked me here to tell you the truth, the way I see it. And now you're arguing with me?"

"No, you're right. You're right. I do want to hear it. Go ahead."

And she did. Over seasonal field greens and quail with parsley sauce, she told him he had never really seen her; he had wanted her around to warm his bed and to look good on his arm when he went out, but he had never wanted to know her. She told him he'd dismissed her interests, indulging them by throwing money at them but never attempting to understand or share them. She told him she'd never felt like she could talk to him about the things that mattered to her, and when she tried, he didn't listen. And she told him she felt like he'd tried to buy her, over and over again.

"I didn't want to remodel Cooper House. Not really. I just wanted to feel comfortable there. I wanted to feel like it was ours instead of just yours. But you thought if you could keep me busy picking paint colors and fabric swatches—"

"That's not what I—"

She reached out and gently placed her index finger on his mouth. "I'm talking and you're listening, remember?"

So he shut up and let her finish.

The picture he got, in the end, was of a woman who'd been trying to reach out to him but who'd hit a brick wall of indifference while he'd tried to distract her with his wealth. The question wasn't why the relationship had failed. The question was, why hadn't it failed sooner?

When she was done, he sat back and took a long swallow of his wine, thinking there wasn't enough wine in the world to make him feel better about everything she'd said.

"I'm sorry," he told her, finally. "If that's how I made you feel, I'm sorry."

"Well." She smiled slightly, those perfectly painted lips curving faintly upward. "It's not worth much now, I suppose, but it's still nice to hear."

CHRIS STAYED at his condo that night and drove home the next day feeling hopeless about his prospects with Martina. If everything Alexis had said was true—and he suspected it was—how could he hope to avoid the same problems this time around?

The thing was, he really liked Martina. He liked her more than he'd liked Alexis, more than he'd ever liked anyone. He didn't want to see this thing with her crash in flames the way every other relationship had done. But how could he avoid it if he didn't even understand himself?

He'd thought a few times that seeing a therapist might be in order. He hated the idea of it—hated the concept of sitting in some over air-conditioned office designed to be soothing, the therapist handing him a box of tissues while he talked about how his mother had failed him.

Which, let's face it, she really had.

Still, it was worth a try, wasn't it?

One nice thing about being wealthy was that he didn't have to jump through the hoops most people did when they wanted to see a healthcare professional. He had people to jump through those hoops for him.

He'd had a full-time personal assistant when he'd had his company. Now that he didn't, she wasn't full-time anymore, but he sometimes called her when he needed something done and didn't have the time or inclination to do it himself.

"Janet, could you find me a good therapist on the Central Coast and make me the first available appointment?" he asked via the Bluetooth in his car as he drove south.

"Of course. What kind of therapist are we talking about? Is your knee acting up again?"

He tried to keep his tone neutral. "Not a physical therapist. A psychologist. Someone who specializes in relationship issues."

"Oh. Certainly. I'll take care of that right away." She sounded entirely too enthusiastic for his taste. "And, I hope I'm not out of line in saying this, but ..."

"Yes?" he prompted her.

"It's about time."

MARTINA MADE it two weeks before she broke down and agreed to see him socially. The construction of his new kitchen had started, so she'd seen him in the context of work, but she'd kept it professional, wanting to give herself time to think.

She'd intended to go longer—not to punish him, but to get some clarity about what she wanted and how she wanted to get it—but she missed him too much.

She hadn't been sleeping well because she couldn't go to bed without feeling how empty it was without him there. That was pathetic, she knew, but it was the truth. She felt sad all the time, and she didn't like feeling sad. That heavy weight of pure loneliness and regret that sat on her chest had to be lifted one way or another.

She called him a couple of days before Sofia's bridal shower.

"So," she said. "I thought maybe we should ... you know. Get together."

"Is this to talk about the kitchen?" He sounded tentative. "Because I don't want to fool myself that you mean something different than that."

"It's not to talk about the kitchen."

~

THEY MET at Madeline's on Main Street for dinner that night, and during the entree, Martina reached out and took his hand on the tabletop amid candlelight and white linen. When they'd finished dinner and she had paid—she'd insisted, and he'd known better than to argue—she invited herself back to his house.

"Are you sure?" He looked impossibly hopeful, and it would have crushed her to disappoint him.

"I'm sure." They went straight to his bedroom, where they both undressed as quickly as they could and then climbed under the covers and into each other's arms.

"I missed you," he said when she pressed her bare body against his.

"I missed you, too."

And then they didn't talk anymore.

~

AFTERWARD, there were issues they needed to work out.

"I can't just let you buy me things—especially not a piece of property," she told him once they were dressed. It was important that she be dressed for this. "When you did that, I just ... I didn't know what to think. And I had to think."

"Okay." He nodded. "But it's about to close escrow. What do you want me to do with it? Put it back on the market?"

"Yes."

"Really."

"Yes, really. And then let somebody else—your accountant or your real estate lawyer or somebody—let them deal with the details of it. When I submit an offer, I don't want it accepted just because it's me. I want you out of it."

He smiled a little, as though he found her amusing. "I can do that."

"I know you *can*. But will you? Will you stay out of it so I can buy the property fair and square? So I can do it on my own, without your help?"

He used his index finger to draw an X over his heart. "I promise. But I'm not sure why you want that. We know someone else wants to make an offer. At least, they made one last time. What if I accidentally accept theirs instead of yours? I could give you a deal. I could—"

"No! God. Aren't you even listening to me?" An anger that was close to despair rose in her. How could this ever work if he didn't listen or, worse, if he tried to listen but didn't understand?

"Yes, Martina. I'm listening. I just don't—"

"Chris. If you don't get why I want to do it this way, that's fine. But it's what I want. Please tell me you'll do it."

"All right. I'll do it."

It wasn't enough for her, and it wasn't fine. But it would have to do for now.

~

CHRIS THOUGHT IT WAS, frankly, nonsensical that Martina wanted him to treat her like anyone else regarding the real estate deal. She wasn't just anyone else. He'd never known anyone who didn't want to take advantage of personal connections when it came to business.

But he'd never known anyone exactly like her, so was it beyond understanding that she might think differently than everyone else he knew?

He'd only seen the therapist a couple of times, so he didn't have much to draw on for insight.

Still, they'd had a few sessions, and the therapist—a trim, middle-aged woman named Karen who would remind him of his mother, if his mother were both sober and insightful—had offered one thing that might be useful here.

Martina's telling you what she needs. Are you hearing her?

Martina and Alexis both had said the same thing—that he didn't listen.

Okay, so he could try to listen. Even if he didn't get why she wanted what she wanted, he could at least believe her when she told him she wanted it.

When escrow closed, he would put the property back on the market, and he would hire someone to handle the transaction for him. He would not be privy to any of the details—like the names of anyone who might make an offer.

And if she didn't get the property because someone else got it first? Or if she paid more than she had to? Fine. If that was what she wanted, then so be it.

God, women were confusing, mysterious creatures.

28

T he day of the wedding shower dawned not with blue skies and birds tweeting merrily in the trees, but with wind, thunder, and a downpour of rain that would have sent Noah—the Biblical one, not the contractor—scurrying onto the ark.

"*Nooo!*" Sofia wailed when she got up that morning and heard the rain pounding on the roof. "Why today? Why does there have to be a giant storm today?"

"It'll be okay," Martina reassured her. "The shower's going to be indoors, so it's going to be fine."

"But people are driving in from out of town! Who wants to drive in this? It's a sign, obviously. I'm not supposed to get married. Not without Mom and Dad here." Tears glimmered in Sofia's eyes.

"Okay, we're not doing that again," Benny said. She was still making her first coffee of the day, and it wasn't a good time to test her patience. She scowled at Sofia. "We're not using Mom and Dad as an excuse for you to get cold feet about marrying Patrick."

"I'm not getting cold feet!" Sofia's literal feet were encased in fuzzy slippers, but her figurative feet did, in fact, seem a bit chilly.

"Bullshit." Benny poured coffee into her mug, took a sip, and sighed in relief.

"Sofia, we've been over all of this." Martina spoke more gently than Benny had. She got up and went to where Sofia was standing at the kitchen island and put her hand on Sofia's shoulder. "Mom and Dad would want you to be happy. They'd love Patrick. They would be over the moon that you're getting married to such a great guy, even if they can't be here to see it."

"And Mom would kick your ass for even thinking about backing out," Benny said.

It was true. If Carmela could be here, she'd be railing about how her daughter was an *idiota* for even thinking about letting such a good man go.

"I'm not thinking of backing out," Sofia said in a small voice. "But why does it have to be raining? Why today?"

"I could give you a lecture about the water cycle and its role in maintaining a healthy ecosystem," Benny said. "But something tells me you weren't asking from a scientific perspective."

"Look. We can ask ourselves why and worry about the people who might not make it here," Martina said, "or we can just accept what is and make this the best day possible for whoever does manage to part the Red Sea and get here."

"That Red Sea thing isn't helping," Sofia said.

"Sorry." Martina massaged Sofia's shoulder a little. "Do you want some herbal tea? It's very soothing."

"I want a shot of whiskey," Sofia said, "but considering it's seven a.m., that's probably out."

"Probably," Martina agreed.

"Not necessarily," Benny added. "If that's what's going to get you through the day without an anxiety meltdown, we can get Bianca over here and have her set it up in an IV drip."

"Funny," Martina said.

"I'll be okay." Sofia wiped her eyes, then grabbed a napkin from the holder on the counter and blew her nose. "I'll be fine."

"What's going on out here?" Patrick came out of the bedroom looking alarmed. "Is everything okay? Sofia? Are you all right?"

"It's the rain," Martina told him.

"Oh." Patrick's brow furrowed as he considered that. "Don't they say it's good luck when it rains on the day of your bridal shower?"

"That's the wedding day!" Sofia said. "Not the bridal shower."

"Well. If we're taking the word *shower* literally—"

"Don't be funny," Sofia said. "Not right now. I swear to God, Patrick—"

"All right, all right," Benny said before the two of them could start to fight—which they never did, really. "Do you want me to call around and cancel it, or do you want to toughen the hell up and make the best of it?" From Benny's tone, there was clearly only one viable option.

"When you put it that way ..." Sofia sniffed.

"It's early," Martina said. "There's still time for the weather to clear up before people from LA or the Bay Area get to the Central Coast. You go and ... I don't know. Take a shower or something. I'll call the restaurant and the bakery and make sure everything's still a go. We've got this. Go on, now." Martina put her hands on Sofia's shoulders, turned her toward her bedroom, and gave her a little shove.

When she was gone, Patrick was still standing there, looking concerned.

"Don't worry," Martina told him. "She's just thinking about Mom and Dad. She's going to be okay."

"Are you sure?"

"*Pfft.*" Benny made a dismissive noise and waved her hand as if to shoo away a fly. "Of course she is. What's she going to do, get in her car and drive to Mexico to avoid marrying you?"

Patrick looked as though he worried she might do exactly that.

"Maybe Patrick's the one who needs that whiskey IV drip," Martina observed.

Martina still had a feeling of buoyant optimism about the shower despite the weather—until she called Neptune to confirm their reservation.

"Oh, I'm so sorry." The woman who'd answered the phone sounded aggrieved.

"About what?"

"There's been a leak. We have to close." At first Martina wasn't sure she'd heard correctly. "I'm sorry.... What?"

"When the prep crew came in this morning, there was two inches of water on the floor in the dining room. We can't open."

"But I have reservations." Martina said it as though that very fact, in itself, could reverse the effects of the weather.

"I know, and I wish there was something we could do, but we have no choice. Even if we could get rid of the water that fast, it would be a safety hazard to open, not to mention a health violation."

Martina looked at her phone as though it had somehow malfunctioned. "But ... two inches of water? It didn't rain *that* much. How ..."

"It wasn't the rain. A pipe broke. We've got a plumber here now, but it's going to be days, maybe longer."

"We're having a bridal shower! People are coming from LA and the Bay Area! They're already on their way! What am I supposed to do?!" Martina felt nearly hysterical.

"I don't know. I can offer you a different date if you want. I can—"

"They're already on their way here!" Martina repeated.

"I'm sorry. I—"

Martina didn't want to hear again how sorry the woman was, so she hung up. She looked around for Benny and found her in her room sorting through a basket of dirty laundry.

"*Psst!*" Martina hissed at her from the doorway.

"What is that noise you're making?" Benny asked irritably.

"I need to tell you something, and I don't want Sofia to hear it!" Martina said in a stage whisper.

"Then come in here and close the door, and just tell me. Unless you want to send it in Morse code."

Martina closed the door, went to Benny, and said in a low voice, "Neptune's underwater. Literally. They're closing. We don't have anywhere to hold the shower."

Benny stopped what she was doing, rubbed her eyes with her

hands, shook her head to clear it, and looked at Martina. "What the hell are you talking about?"

Martina explained about the pipe, the leak, and the two inches of water. Then she said, "We're going to have to call everyone and tell them to come here instead."

"Oh, shit." Benny put a hand on her hip. "We've got, what, thirty people coming? We don't have room for that many people here. Plus, Sofia's going to say it's not part of Mom's plan. It's not in the binder, so ..."

"I know it's not in the binder! But the binder never said anything about a broken pipe at Neptune!"

"Okay. Okay. Let's think." Benny sat down heavily on the side of her bed. "The binder never said Neptune specifically. It just said the bridal shower should be someplace special, someplace elegant."

"Right. So ..."

"So, we just need to find someplace special and elegant," Benny said.

"For today," Martina reminded her. "For thirty people. With pretty much zero notice."

"Well, I didn't say it was going to be easy. I just said it's what we need!"

"Okay. Okay. We'll start calling places. But in the meantime, we need to make sure Sofia doesn't know about any of this until we've got it fixed. She's already freaking out because of the weather."

"Right." Benny went to her bedroom door, opened it, and called out, "Hey, Patrick? Could you come in here a minute?"

Patrick came in, looking a bit nervous about being in Benny's bedroom, as though her delicate unmentionables might spring out of their drawers and attack him.

"Here's the deal." Benny told him about the Neptune situation, about their plan to find another venue, and about the necessity of keeping Sofia in the dark until they had a workable solution to present to her.

"We need you to get her out of here," Martina said. "Take her to the movies. Take her shopping. Take her ... anywhere. Preferably somewhere with no cell phone service. Or WiFi. Or any other possible way for her to hear the news about Neptune."

To his credit, Patrick didn't panic. He simply nodded, got a grim look of determination on his face, and said, "I'm on it." He left the room, and about twenty minutes later, Benny and Martina heard him and Sofia leaving the house.

"All right," Martina said when they were gone. "Let's work the problem. Start calling restaurants. I'll take letters A through L, you take M through Z."

THEY STARTED CALLING, and they got in touch with Bianca so she could help. They assigned Bianca out-of-town venues in case they couldn't find anything in Cambria, but they all hoped it wouldn't come to that.

By the time Martina had contacted five restaurants in the A through L category, she had already begun to lose hope. Most of the restaurants in Cambria were fairly small, so absorbing a last-minute party of thirty was next to impossible. The ones that did have larger rooms offered a little more hope, but it was a weekend and therefore a big tourist day. Everybody expressed sympathy when Martina told them what was going on, but so far, nobody had been able to help.

She was starting to think they would just have to cram everyone into their own house and feed them food from the freezer section at Albertson's when Chris called.

"Hey." He had a smile in his voice, as though Martina's world were not currently coming apart. "How's your day going?"

She unloaded on him. "My day? It sucks, thanks. My day totally sucks. And Sofia's is going to suck, too, when I tell her that her shower isn't happening." She was on the verge of tears, and she struggled to tamp them down.

"Oh, no. What's going on?"

She told him about Neptune and the water leak and about her

failed efforts to find an alternative location for the event. The part about the weather, he presumably already knew.

"She's already freaking out because Mom and Dad can't be here to see her get married. This is going to send her over the edge." Martina, herself, felt pretty close to the edge at the moment.

"Why not have it here?" he asked.

Martina was silent while the surprise of that hit her. "What, you mean at Cooper House?"

"Sure. Why not? There's plenty of room, and it's different. It's not the same old, same old."

She thought about it. Cooper House was a local legend. Sofia had never been there, so it would be new to her. The place was like a mini Hearst Castle—the guests would likely be awed.

"Are you serious? Really?"

"Of course I'm serious. You could have it in the ballroom."

"You have a ballroom?" She'd never seen the full house; there was an entire wing she'd never had occasion to visit.

"A small one."

Who had a small ballroom in their house that their significant other had never even seen? Chris, that was who. No one else, probably.

"Oh, my God. That would be ... That's great. Thank you so much. You're a lifesaver."

"No problem." He sounded pleased to have made her happy, and that lit a little fire in her chest that made her want to hold him, to kiss him.

"Oh."

"What?"

"Well ... there's still the issue of food. Neptune was going to provide the food, and now—"

"That one, I don't have an answer for," he said.

WHEN MARTINA TOLD Benny about Chris's offer to use Cooper House,

Benny pumped her fist in triumph. "Woo! That's awesome. I'm surprised we didn't think to ask him."

"It's good, right?" Martina asked. "People will like it."

"Aunt Louisa will crap her pants. She will literally crap her pants."

Martina wasn't sure that was a good thing, but Benny said it as though it were.

"But there's still the issue of the food," Martina said. "I mean, Neptune was going to do that. And now ..."

"We'll make it work," Benny said. "If we have to serve everyone Swanson's chicken nuggets and Saltines, we'll make it work."

29

T he chicken nuggets and Saltines didn't turn out to be necessary. Instead, Bianca offered to make a big meal for the invitees.

"But you're pregnant!" Martina exclaimed when Bianca made the offer.

"I've noticed."

"I just meant ... are you up to it? You're huge."

"I won't take offense, even though you said that as though I'm a carnival freakshow exhibit," Bianca said.

"I'm sorry. I didn't mean—"

Bianca proceeded as though Martina hadn't spoken. "I've got less than a week until my due date. I need something to keep my mind off counting the days until the baby comes. Besides, I'm not running a marathon. I'm just making some pasta."

"Okay. Thank you. Oh, but ..."

"Yes?"

"The kitchen at Cooper House is in the middle of renovations, so you're going to have to do as much as you can at home."

Bianca was silent for a moment. Then: "The way things are going, that figures."

"There's a functioning oven and stove. And there's running water. It's just kind of a mess because the countertops and the cabinetry are being redone. Oh, God. Is this a bad idea? Should we just cancel?" Martina was starting to panic.

"No, we shouldn't cancel. If there's running water and a stove and an oven, we'll be fine. Oh, wait. Is there a refrigerator?"

"Yes! A big one."

"Fine. We can do this."

"Okay. I'll let Chris know."

MARTINA ALSO HAD to alert the baker, who had been told to bring the cake to Neptune. With that done, she and Benny started calling the guests to let them know the change of venue.

They were able to reach most of the guests on their cell phones as they drove. But a few people weren't reachable, maybe because their cell phones were out of battery power, or maybe because they were on the road in a part of the state that didn't get good cell service. Martina called Neptune and asked them to put a sign on the door telling shower guests to go to Cooper House instead and giving them the address and driving directions.

"Ooh. You're having it at Cooper House?" The same woman Martina had talked to earlier now sounded both intrigued and impressed. "How did you swing that?"

"Oh. Christopher Mills is my ... ah ... friend." She couldn't quite bring herself to say the word *boyfriend*.

"God, I wish I could see that place," she said. "I don't suppose you could add another person to the guest list?"

"Oh. I ..."

"Just kidding. I have to be here to help clean up this mess. God, life is fun, isn't it?"

MARTINA, Benny, and Bianca got to Cooper House early to organize things before the event. They toted wrapped gifts, plastic shopping bags full of decorations, and ingredients for Bianca's meal, reasoning they could get more of whatever they needed once they realized what it was.

When they arrived, Chris met them at the door. He ushered them into the living room—the room that would have been called the parlor when the house was built—where a small team of people was busy cleaning, setting up flower arrangements, and rearranging furniture to accommodate a buffet-style meal setup.

"I thought about the ballroom idea, but Cynthia"—he gestured toward the woman who appeared to be in charge of the work being done—"thought we'd be better off doing it in here."

"More intimate," Cynthia said over her shoulder as she straightened the linen on a large table that had been set up on one side of the room. "Plus, with the rain, it'll be nice to have the fireplace."

At one end of the room, a fire was burning cheerfully in the hearth. Cynthia was right. It was nice.

"You did all this?" Martina asked Chris. "Just in the time since I called you?"

"I didn't do it. Cynthia did."

"But ... how did you ..."

"Alexis had a few parties here," Chris said, as though he was embarrassed to be bringing up his ex's name. "Cynthia planned them. It just happened that she was available today, so ..." He gestured expansively toward the room and all that was happening in it.

"That's amazing." Impulsively, Martina threw her arms around Cynthia, who laughed in surprise.

"What about me?" Chris asked.

"You, I've got more than a hug for." Her voice was seductive.

"Oh, boy," Benny said. "You two want us to leave so you can have the room?"

"Shut up," Martina said.

BIANCA HAD AN EASIER time cooking in the half-dismantled kitchen than they had expected. Because all of the major appliances were in place and working, all she needed was a decent work space. Chris, Benny, and Martina hauled a table from the formal dining room into the kitchen, and that became Bianca's command central.

Benny, working as sous-chef, chopped tomatoes for sauce while Bianca browned Italian sausage and chunks of beef.

"What can I do?" Martina asked them.

"You can call Patrick and ask him how things are going with Sofia," Bianca suggested. "Tell him we're running on schedule but that he should not—I repeat, he should *not*—get her here early. If she sees this kitchen, she's going to blow a gasket."

"Right. I've got it." Martina went into the next room to talk on the phone because she didn't want Sofia to overhear any of the chaos if she should somehow be the one to answer the phone.

Fortunately, Patrick picked up.

"How's it going? Are you keeping her distracted?" Martina asked.

"Mostly. But she keeps wanting to call you to check in. So far I've managed to put her off, but I don't know how much longer I can keep her away from a phone. I've managed to lose hers between the car's seat cushions, but she's bound to find it soon."

"Well, if she calls, I'll have a story ready."

"Good. And, Martina?"

"*Hmm?*"

"Thank you. For everything. I know you're going through hell to make sure this shower happens, and I ... Well. It just means a lot to me." The sincerity in Patrick's voice made Martina smile. She was going to see that Sofia married him even if she had to force her down the aisle at knifepoint.

Hopefully, it wouldn't come to that.

"She's lucky to have you, Patrick. Really. We all are." She was starting to get choked up, and they couldn't have that on top of everything else, so Martina ended the call before she started getting all sentimental in a way that would require tissues and a retouching of her eye makeup.

Sofia really was lucky to have Patrick—so lucky. And Martina was wondering if maybe she was luckier to have Chris than she'd realized. Yes, they'd had some issues about his money and the relative power imbalance it created. But look what he'd done for her—for her sisters. Look at the trouble he'd gone through to solve their problem and make sure the day went well. He hadn't had to do any of it, and yet he hadn't hesitated. She planned to thank him properly later, when they were alone. Until then, she simply marveled at his easy generosity.

She went back into the kitchen and reported to her sisters that all was well with Sofia for the moment. But Sofia was getting restless and wanted to check in.

"Well, we'd better make sure that when she does, we've only got positive things to tell her," Bianca said. "Here, Martina. Start making the salad."

30

B y the time the guests began to arrive, the rain had let up a little. The fire was burning in the fireplace, the room was warm and inviting, and Cynthia's tasteful and understated decorations made the room festive and lovely.

Patrick had waited to tell Sofia about the change in plans until they were on their way to Cooper House. At first she had panicked, Patrick reported, but once she arrived and saw the house, the decorations, and the food, she calmed down and began to enjoy the day.

"I'm amazed," Patrick told Martina, Bianca, and Benny as he looked around at the party preparations. "I can't believe you managed to pull this together. And so well. This is probably going to be better than if it had gone according to the original plan."

Martina thought so, too. Cooper House rarely got used by groups of people—at least, by anyone other than Alexis—and the house clearly had been made to provide hospitality, to accommodate large groups for social occasions. Martina looked around with satisfaction as Russo relatives and Sofia's friends talked, drank, and mingled contentedly in front of the fireplace.

Martina went to Sofia to check on her.

"Oh, my God, thank you. I can't believe it. You really saved the day." Sofia's eyes were glimmering with unshed tears of happiness. "When Patrick told me about Neptune—"

"We didn't want you to know until you had to know," Martina said. "We thought you'd freak out and say it was a sign."

"I would have," she admitted.

"Well, it *is* a sign," Martina said. "It's a sign that whatever comes up, we can handle it."

"You can. Thank you so much." Sofia gave Martina a big, tight hug before going to greet some guests who had just come in.

MARTINA MADE THE ROUNDS, checking on everything and seeing things were under control. She popped her head into the kitchen to ask if there was anything she could do to help with the food.

"Everything under control in here?" she asked.

"Yes." Bianca's face looked tight as she stood over a pot of sauce, stirring and tasting.

"Are you sure?" Martina frowned. "You don't look so great."

"Thanks. That's flattering."

"That's not what I mean. It's just ... You don't look like you feel that great."

"I'm fine," Bianca said. "Could you check on the garlic bread?"

THE REST of the event went well. Guests from out of town found Cooper House without incident, no one got into an accident on the rainy roads, no one got excessively drunk, and the food was excellent. Sofia opened her gifts, exclaiming over the crystal candlesticks, the Italian linens, and the occasional off-color gag gift suggesting what Sofia and Patrick might or might not get up to on the wedding night.

Sofia glowed, not just because she was beautiful—which she was —but because she was happy. Patrick made her happy.

"I'm glad she's marrying you." Martina gave Patrick's arm a

squeeze as they watched Sofia open the gifts. It wasn't traditional for the groom to be at the wedding shower, but Patrick had wanted to share in the excitement, and who was going to tell him no?

"I'm glad, too," he said.

HALFWAY THROUGH THE GIFT-OPENING, when the lunch dishes were being cleared away and the cake was being set up on the table, Martina looked around the room and frowned.

"Where's Bianca?" she asked Benny.

"When she finished cooking, she said she needed to lie down for a bit. I think Chris put her in one of the guest bedrooms."

There were so many of those, Martina thought, it could take all day to find her.

"Is she okay?" Martina asked. "Earlier, I thought she looked a little pale."

"She cooked for thirty while carrying around eight pounds of unborn baby. I'd be pale, too."

Fair enough. Still, Martina was worried, and she left the parlor to poke around a little, looking for her sister.

She didn't find Bianca, but she found Chris in his study.

"Hey." She waggled her fingers at him from the doorway.

"Oh. Hi. How are things going out there?"

"Great." She went to where he was sitting at his desk and lowered herself onto his lap, putting her arms around his neck.

"What's this for? Not that I'm complaining."

"Thank you." She kissed him. "You saved us. Really. You might even have saved Sofia's wedding. You didn't have to do all of this, but I'm so glad you did."

He lowered his eyes, looking embarrassed but also pleased. "You're welcome."

"By the way. Have you seen Bianca? Benny said she wasn't feeling well, and you let her use a guest bedroom."

"Yeah. She said she was tired and needed to lie down. I showed her to the downstairs bedroom next to the gym." His brow furrowed. "Is she okay?"

"Oh, I'm sure she is. I was just looking for her, that's all."

MARTINA CHECKED the bedroom Chris had mentioned. She found that the bedcover was mussed, as though someone had been lying on it, but Bianca wasn't there. Well, maybe she'd felt better and had returned to the party.

Martina checked there, but again, no Bianca.

"I can't find her," she told Benny in the living room as Benny stood with a plate of cake and a fork in her hand.

"Who, Bianca?"

"Yeah. Chris said he put her in a guest bedroom to rest, but she's not there."

Benny shrugged. "Maybe she's in the can. Pregnant women have to pee a lot. So I'm told."

"Maybe." But a quick check of several downstairs bathrooms yielded no Bianca.

Martina dug her cell phone out of her purse and called her.

"What?" Bianca answered. Her voice sounded tense, and Martina could hear traffic sounds in the background.

"Where are you?" Martina asked. "I've been looking everywhere. Are you even still at Cooper House?"

"No, I am not."

"Bianca—"

"Don't you dare tell Sofia this," Bianca said, "but I'm on my way to the hospital to have the baby."

"*What?!*"

"The contractions started when I was in the middle of making the meat sauce. I held off as long as I could, but then my water broke."

"Oh, my God. You're not driving, are you?"

"Of course not. I'm not an idiot." Bianca made some kind of

gasping sound that made Martina's pulse race. "I called TJ. He picked me up."

"Holy shit. Where are you now?"

"We're"—she groaned—"We're on the 46 headed for the hospital in Templeton. I swear to God I will kill you with my bare hands if you tell Sofia and ruin her party. We've—oh, shit, this hurts—we've got this under control."

"Let me talk to TJ."

"Martina—"

"Let me talk to TJ right now."

TJ came on the phone, his voice tense but businesslike. "Yep."

"TJ, is she okay?"

"I think so. We should be there soon."

"All right. Do you need anything? Is there anything I can do?"

"Not unless you can teleport here and get us there faster."

She couldn't do that, obviously. In fact, she was hard pressed to think of anything helpful she could offer at this moment.

"Are you sure we shouldn't all come out there? Not everyone, obviously, but me, Sofia, and Benny?"

"No!" Bianca yelled from the background. "TJ, tell her no. Finish the party, then come out."

"You heard her," TJ said.

"Oh, God."

"Look," TJ said. "There's nothing you can do. We're almost at the hospital. It's going to be fine. Just get here when you can."

KEEPING her mouth shut about Bianca was one of the hardest things Martina had ever done. She didn't even tell Benny, because she was pretty sure Benny would have an even harder time being quiet about it than she would.

When the last gift was opened, the last piece of cake was eaten, the last cocktail was finished, and the last guest had been thanked and ushered off to her home or hotel room, Martina turned to her sisters, Patrick, and Chris, who had come downstairs when things began to wind down.

"Okay, do not freak out when I tell you what I'm about to tell you." Martina tried to remain calm and matter-of-fact, her voice steady. "Bianca is on her way to the hospital. Her water broke. She's having the baby."

"Ha, ha. That's a good one." Sofia, still glowing from the triumph of her party, laughed.

"Oh, shit. She's not kidding," Benny said.

A certain amount of pandemonium broke out in the wake of the announcement. Everyone started talking at once, and people were running around looking for their coats and purses so they could rush out of the house.

"Wait. Wait!" Martina held up her hands to get everyone's attention. "I talked to TJ, and he said everything's okay. Of course, he was speeding to the hospital while he said it, so, grain of salt."

"Why didn't you tell me? You should have told me!" Sofia ran her hands through her hair, looking panicked.

"Bianca didn't want that. In fact, she said, and I quote, 'I will kill you with my bare hands if you tell Sofia.' So."

"We have to get to the hospital! We have to go!" Benny said.

If Martina had predicted who was going to emerge as the leader in this scenario, she might have said it would be Benny, who was a take-charge person in general, or Patrick, who managed to control a classroom full of undergrads on a daily basis.

She would not have predicted it would be Chris, who had come down to join the group when Martina couldn't find her sister.

"Okay, listen up," he said, suddenly commanding the attention of everyone in the room. "My SUV is big enough for all of us. I'm the person least likely to lose his shit in this situation, so I'll drive."

Martina looked around. "But your house." The place was a shambles, with used plates and glasses, torn wrapping paper, and the detritus of the party littering the space around them.

"I'll have the caretaker deal with it."

"He has a caretaker," Benny remarked, smirking.

"You want to offer some sort of social commentary, or do you want to get there before the baby's in grade school?" Martina said.

"Good point. Where's the car?"

THE DRIVE to Templeton didn't usually seem like a long one—just thirty minutes over a scenic highway overlooking rolling green hills with the Pacific Ocean lying still and blue in the distance—but today, it seemed to take forever.

"Can't you make this thing move faster?" Benny prodded Chris from her seat in the back.

"I can, but I assume we want to get there in the SUV and not in the back of an ambulance." He was already going eighty.

"Good point," Patrick said.

Martina had called TJ, and he'd reported they had arrived safely and Bianca was in a delivery room.

"Have they at least given her an epidural yet?" Martina wanted to know.

"They told her she can't have one. It's too late. She knew it would be—she's a doctor—but she still didn't take it all that well."

TJ must have been right there in the delivery room, because Martina could hear Bianca in the background. "I didn't want to do it this way!" she moaned. "I wanted the goddamned drugs!"

"Oh, boy," Martina said.

THEY GOT TO THE HOSPITAL, and Chris pulled up in front of the front doors. Everyone poured out of the SUV and ran inside while Chris parked the car.

They were directed to the labor and delivery unit, where Benny ran up to the nurse's station and accosted a woman in light blue scrubs.

"Where's my sister? Bianca Russo."

"Ah. Dr. Russo." Of course they knew her here—Bianca had privileges at the hospital and came in from time to time to check on her pediatrics patients, including the occasional newborn. "She's in recovery, down the hall."

"Recovery?" Martina said. "We're too late?"

"Too late for the screaming," the nurse said, "but right on time if you want to see the baby."

31

W hen they entered the room, Bianca was in bed looking exhausted and cuddling her son, and TJ was standing by looking both stunned and thrilled.

"That was some way to get out of cleaning up after the party," Benny remarked, looking down at the red, pinched newborn in Bianca's arms. "You could have just said, *Hey, I did the cooking. You take care of it.*"

"Very funny." Bianca smiled up at her sister. "Look at him. Isn't he beautiful?"

"He's gorgeous." Martina felt the sting of tears in her eyes as she looked at the baby.

"Where's Owen?" Sofia asked.

"He's with his mother this weekend," TJ said. "I called him to tell him the news. He's over the moon. He's always wanted a little brother he could lord it over."

"I'll bet he can't wait to meet ... What's the baby's name?" Martina asked.

Bianca and TJ had chosen a name months before, but either out of superstition or a desire not to have their choice second-guessed, they'd decided not to tell anyone the name until the birth.

"Everybody, meet Aldo James Davenport," Bianca said. "We're going to call him AJ."

"Oh, my God. You named him after Dad." Tears spilled out of Sofia's eyes.

"And he's got my middle name," TJ said proudly.

"Congratulations, man." Chris extended a hand to shake TJ's, and TJ, who barely knew Chris, took the hand and pulled him into a hug. It was that kind of day.

"Seriously. Congratulations to both of you." Patrick hugged TJ, too, then stood with his hands in his pockets, smiling, clearly pleased. "I can't wait for Sofia to have our first baby."

"Our *first*?" Sofia gaped at Patrick. "How many do you think we're going to have? We talked about one."

"I'm just keeping my options open," Patrick said.

After a while, Bianca consented to let her sisters hold the baby— after everyone had washed their hands. Sofia went first, probably because she was the most likely to have the next baby, and then Martina.

Martina held AJ as though she were afraid he would shatter into a million pieces if she did something wrong. The baby lay in her arms with his little eyes squeezed shut, his lips pursed. He made sounds— a kind of *mmf mmf mmf*—as his lips worked. He was probably remembering his last meal and the various joys it had provided.

"Oh, my goodness," Martina cooed, looking down into his tiny face. "You're so beautiful. Oh, AJ. Your mommy and daddy love you so much. And your Aunt Martina does, too." She was lost in the sensation of holding the warm bundle, smelling his delicious baby smell, feeling his weight in her arms—and imagining the day when she'd have one of her own.

Then she did something that, in retrospect, she wished she could take back. In fact, she wished she could go back in time and sew her own lips shut to save herself from this moment.

"Could you ever imagine yourself having a little one like this?" she asked Chris, so enveloped in bliss that she'd, apparently, lost her mind.

"Oh, hell no," he said.

All chatter in the room died.

"No?"

"Well ... no." He rubbed at the stubble on his chin. "It's not something I can imagine, actually."

"Oh, boy," Benny said in the same voice one might use to say, *There's a deadly asteroid headed toward Earth.*

"What?" Chris asked, as though he didn't realize he'd just stepped in a pile of metaphorical shit so deep and foul that he might never extract himself.

"Here. You'd better take him." Martina gave AJ back to Bianca because she didn't want to dissolve into tears in front of everyone. "I just have to ... to go use the ladies' room." Then she fled the room before anyone could ask her if she was okay.

WHEN CHRIS HAD SAID what he'd said, he hadn't thought there was anything wrong with it. No, he couldn't imagine having a baby. Was that so wrong?

Then, at everyone's reaction, he suspected he had somehow made a terrible mistake.

"Oh, God," he muttered, looking awkwardly at Martina's family, all of whom—except for the baby—were looking at him with undisguised horror.

"I'm guessing I shouldn't have said that."

"Gee. You think?" Benny smirked at him.

"But ... we're new. It's new! I'm supposed to be thinking about babies?" It was all incomprehensible to him—especially the speed with which things had gone from good to complete shit.

"No, you're not supposed to be thinking about babies," Sofia said. "Not in any concrete, planning-for-the-immediate-future kind of way."

"Then ..."

"But you're not supposed to act like she'd suggested handling plutonium with your bare hands," Benny supplied.

"I didn't do that. Did I?"

"Dude, you kind of did," TJ said.

Benny put a hand on Chris's arm—a gesture friendly enough to make him grateful they hadn't all turned on him. "You were great today. Really great. So I'm going to take pity on you and tell you what you did wrong."

"I'd appreciate it." It was like a lifeline, like someone pulling him out of shark-infested waters.

"Martina doesn't want to marry you and have your babies, so you don't have to worry about that. But with how things have been going with the two of you, she's starting to wonder if she might, someday, want to *start thinking* about marrying you and having your babies. Some day in the future. And what you said to her, with your 'Oh, hell no,' was that you not only aren't thinking that way, but you're determined to *never* think that way, not ever, even if the two of you should turn out to be the last male-female pair alive on an otherwise desolate planet."

Was that really what she thought? That not only was he not serious about her, but he would never, under any circumstances, even consider becoming serious about her?

"I didn't intend it that way," he said. "At all. It just ... popped out."

"But did you mean it?" Bianca asked. "About never wanting kids? Because if you did, that's something you two need to talk about sooner rather than later."

"But why?" None of this was making sense to him. "We're just dating. We're not engaged. We're not even living together. We're not there yet."

"Right. But if going there eventually is never going to be on the table for you, you need to tell her. She's in her thirties, and the clock is ticking. She doesn't have forever to find someone. And she does want kids," Sofia told him, not unkindly.

Chris didn't understand why such life-altering decisions had to be made now, when he and Martina were just getting to know each other, when they were just getting used to sharing a bed and being a part of each other's lives. Was it really critical that he know now whether he wanted to father her children?

"This is a lot." He rubbed his forehead, where he could feel the beginnings of a headache.

"I'm going to see if she's okay." Benny shot Chris a look and headed out of the room.

"I didn't mean—" Chris began.

"We know you didn't," Sofia said. "But whether you meant to or not, you did it."

BENNY FOUND MARTINA IN THE LADIES' room down the hall. She was standing in front of a mirror, dabbing at her eyes, trying not to smear her eye makeup. She sniffled and dabbed, sniffled and dabbed, her face red and blotchy. When she saw Benny come in, she let in a ragged breath.

"I'm being an idiot," she said.

"There's an idiot in this equation, for sure, but it's not you," Benny said.

"We haven't been seeing each other all that long," Martina said.

"He said that."

"And there's no reason he should even be thinking in those terms yet."

"He said that, too."

"But ... I'm not getting any younger, and if he's never going to want kids, I need to consider whether I'm wasting my time," Martina said.

"Sofia said that," Benny told her.

"Well, you covered a lot of ground while I was gone."

"He's a guy. When you got upset and ran out, he practically had cartoon question marks floating around over his head. He needed someone to decode it for him."

"But why does he need things to be decoded?" Martina sniffled. "Why are men such idiots?"

"Ah, a question for the ages," Benny said. "If you can answer that one, you'll change not only the experience of love and romance, but you'll also fix politics, war, and the fact that you can't get plastic wrap to stay flat long enough to wrap anything."

Martina gave Benny a courtesy laugh, just to show she appreciated her sister's attempt to lighten the mood.

"So, you're really in love with him, huh?" Benny asked after a while. "I mean, if you weren't, you wouldn't care whether he wants to have babies with you."

A woman in scrubs and a white coat came into the ladies' room and went into a stall. Martina lowered her voice. "I didn't think I was. I really didn't. I thought we were just having a good time. But now ... I guess I need to re-evaluate my feelings and whether it's worth going forward."

Benny gave her a meaningful look. "For what it's worth, Martina, he was really awesome today. I mean, from the way he saved the shower to the way he took charge when we found out about Bianca ... I was impressed. And I'm not easily impressed."

That was true. Chris had been magnificent. But that was part of the problem, wasn't it? It was part of what made Martina upset that he didn't want her babies. If he'd been annoying, useless, or even mediocre today when she'd really needed him, she probably would have taken his comment in stride.

"He really was great," Martina admitted, giving the area under her eyes one last careful blot with a tissue, then turning to her sister. "You know, it wouldn't matter so much to me that he doesn't want kids if he weren't so ... If he didn't have so much ..."

Benny nodded. "I don't even need you to finish those thoughts. He's got so much potential, you started to see white picket fences and baby car seats and golden wedding anniversaries. And then he ruined it all by acting as though having kids would be the same as skydiving without a parachute."

"Yeah, I guess," Martina admitted. "It's stupid."

"It's no more stupid than any of the rest of us falling for some fool who doesn't deserve us." Benny shrugged. "We're women. It's what we do."

The woman in the stall came out and washed her hands, shooting Benny and Martina surreptitious looks. She headed for the door, then turned back hesitantly. "You know, my husband didn't want kids at first. Said he hated children. Wouldn't even consider it."

"So, what happened?" Martina asked.

"I got pregnant on accident." She smiled. "He's a stay-at-home dad now so I can finish my residency. He's the one our daughter wants when she wakes up scared in the middle of the night, and he's the one who cried the last time she had a cold because he couldn't stand to see her uncomfortable." She shrugged. "It's something to think about."

～

MARTINA HAD herself put back together by the time she came out of the restroom and returned to Bianca's room. She'd recovered from the hurt and surprise of what Chris had said—mostly—and she was intent on acting as though nothing had happened.

"Is everything okay?" Chris asked tentatively as Martina came back into the room.

"Fine." Martina smiled. "Bianca, can I hold the baby one more time before we go?"

～

THE DRIVE HOME was awkward as hell for Chris. He had a car full of people who were trying not to say the wrong thing, and Martina was acting as though she were trying to sell solar panels to a reluctant homeowner. Her manner was cheerful, polite—and completely superficial.

"Wasn't AJ adorable?" Martina said to no one in particular. "And Bianca named him after Dad—what a wonderful tribute."

"It really was," Sofia agreed.

Chris might have expected Sofia to say more about it, but she didn't. He got the sense that she, like everyone else, found it hard to talk while being suffocated by the tension in the car.

"Thank you for driving us, Chris," Patrick said, maybe a little too formally.

"My pleasure. I'm glad I could do it." And, hell, could he be any more stiff and awkward himself? Could any of them?

"Bianca will need help in the next few weeks," Martina said. "Meals, that sort of thing. We can set up a schedule."

"That's a good idea," Sofia said.

"I can help," Patrick added. "I make a pretty good mac and cheese."

"Oh, for Christ's sake," Chris said.

Martina looked at him impassively. "You have a problem with mac and cheese?"

"No. I do not have a problem with mac and cheese. I fucking love mac and cheese."

"Okay. I guess we're good on the mac and cheese, then," Patrick said.

"Then what's your issue?" Martina's voice remained calm, polite, and neutral.

"My problem is that nobody really wants to talk about mac and cheese or meal schedules. What you all want to talk about is that I said I don't want children, and Martina had to flee the room to cry. That's what you really want to talk about." Chris was probably shooting himself in the metaphorical foot by putting it all out there, but he would rather deal with the issue head-on rather than making painful chitchat the rest of the ride home.

"Well, sure," Benny said. "But we're not talking about that because we didn't want you to hurl yourself out of a moving vehicle. Especially because you're driving."

Everyone waited for Martina to say something, since she was, after all, at the center of this.

"Not now," she said, when she finally spoke.

"What?" Chris said.

"I said, not now. We'll talk about it, if you want to, but not at this exact moment. Not while we're in a car full of people and not while I'm supposed to be enjoying the glow of new aunthood. Not. Now." Her tone made it clear he'd be a fool to try pressing forward with the topic, so he closed his mouth and focused on the road.

"About that meal schedule," Sofia said.

MARTINA HAD SAID they would talk about it later, when they were alone, but by the time they were alone, she no longer wanted to talk to Chris about this or anything else.

When they got to Cooper House, they all helped Sofia and Patrick load the shower gifts into their car. Sofia and Patrick headed home, then Benny got into her own car and headed back to the Russo house.

For a few minutes, Martina wasn't sure what she was going to do —whether she was going to get into her Prius and follow them or go inside and have The Talk with Chris about their future and whether they even had one.

But the thought of having that talk was exhausting after a day that had been problematic from the start. So, instead of going inside, she headed toward her car, her bag slung over her shoulder, her mood grim.

"You're going?" Chris stuffed his hands into the pockets of his pants.

"I am. Unless you need me to come inside and clean up from the party."

He waved her off. "I'm sure it's done by now. Graham texted me an hour ago and said he was on it. So ... we're fine."

Martina wished she had a caretaker who could clean up the mess of her personal life as easily as he could clear away the remains of a bridal shower.

"Okay, then. I'm going to go home and get some rest."

"All right. If you want me to drive you—"

"I'm fine."

"Martina?"

She stopped and looked back at him.

"Are we okay?"

Her first instinct was to reassure him—to tell him yes, they were fine, and what he'd said didn't really matter. But she didn't have it in her to make him feel better for making her feel like shit.

"I'll call you tomorrow about the kitchen." Then she got into her car and drove home.

32

C hris was sure he could make things right on Monday when Martina called to talk about the remodel. By then, she'd have had some time to think things over. That's all she really needed, surely. Then he could apologize and they could move on as though his ill-fated remark had never been said.

But when she called, she was all business. She spoke to him not about their relationship, such as it was, but about work schedules and inspection reports.

"Martina, forget about the kitchen for a minute," he told her, becoming increasingly frustrated. "About that thing I said—"

"We don't have to talk about that."

"But I want to apologize."

She was silent for a moment. "About what?"

"Well ... about what I said."

"What I mean is, do you want to apologize because what you said isn't true? Or because it is true, and you're sorry I was upset by it?"

It was a fair enough question, and he considered it carefully before answering. "It was true. It was my honest reaction to the idea of having kids. But I'm sorry about the way it came out and the timing of it. And I'm sorry it upset you."

"Okay. That's fair. Thank you for the apology." But then she started talking about the kitchen again, and he could see he was still screwed.

He tried again over the next few days as the work on his kitchen was being finished. The cabinets and countertops were in, and the painters were taking care of the final details, like the crown molding and the other trim. Martina came over at the end of the day to inspect it and give him an update on their progress.

"Okay, I've checked with the painting crew, and they're going to do another coat tomorrow. After that, we should be finished. I'll send you the final invoice once that's done. Unless there's anything you're dissatisfied with that needs extra attention." They were in Chris's study, him sitting behind his desk, her standing formally in the middle of the room, her hands folded together at her waist.

"Martina, stop it."

Her eyebrows rose delicately. "Stop what?"

"Stop acting as though I'm just another client. We need to talk about this."

"We already have."

"Okay, then why are you acting like this?"

"Like what?" He saw a hint of pain pass over her features, and he felt sorry for it.

"Like you're some stranger who's only here to polish my grout. I don't want this. I don't want us to be like this. I want to talk about it."

Her shoulders sagged, and she dropped her professional persona. "I'm sorry. I don't want to be difficult. I'm just trying to sort out whether it's even worth talking about."

He felt gut-punched. How could this—the two of them—not be worth the effort to fix whatever was wrong?

"I don't know what you mean," he said.

Her face was starting to look red and pained, and he realized with horror that she was trying to hold back tears. "It's just ... you told me the truth about how you feel. And that's fine. It's ... it's good you told me the truth. But now that I know, I don't know if we should pursue this."

"Martina, I don't think it's right for you to punish me because of how I feel about kids."

"I'm not punishing you." Now a couple of stray tears did fall, and she wiped them from her cheeks impatiently. "It's not about punishing anyone. It's about me trying to find a way to have the life I want. And part of what I want is children. I didn't realize how much until I saw Bianca with AJ. If you don't want the same things, then I can't fault you for that. It's just who you are. But, between that and the money—"

"What are you talking about? What about the money?" He got up and walked to her. He was beginning to think this was worse than he'd suspected.

"When you bought the Hall property, thinking to give it to me ... Chris, that wasn't just a misstep. It wasn't just something you thought I might want that I really didn't. It was a statement."

"A statement," he said.

"Yes. It was a statement about who you are and what your values are, and I can see they're very different from mine. I just don't know if we're compatible enough, and I don't know if it's something we can overcome."

He ran a hand through his hair, feeling that this thing was growing increasingly out of his control. "I thought we'd settled that. I thought—"

"We settled the question of what to do with the property. But we didn't settle the issue of you being the kind of person who thinks you can buy your way into someone's life."

He searched his mind for something useful from his therapy sessions—something he could draw forth to make this situation better. But, hell, his therapist had said something similar to him— that he tried to buy people's love and attention. Was it true? Was that what he did?

"Do I do that?" He was bewildered by it, just as he had been when Karen had said it to him. "Do I really do that?"

"I don't want it," she said. "I don't want our relationship to be all about what you can buy for me or what I can get you to give me.

It's just not something I know how to handle. Chris, it's not who I am."

He could see that. Wasn't it the very thing that had made Martina so different from the other women he'd been with? Wasn't the most alluring thing about Martina that she was more interested in what she could give than in what she could get? The very idea of someone being oriented that way had been a revelation to him. And he didn't want to let her go.

He put a hand on her shoulder, but she stepped back out of his grasp.

"Isn't there something I can do to fix this?" he said softly.

"I don't know. I don't think so. Because it's about the basic essence of who we are as people. How can you fix that?"

MARTINA WENT HOME and had a good cry, lying face down on her bed. She'd wanted so much to fall into his arms and let him hold her. She'd wanted to kiss him, to take him by the hand and lead him to his bed. She'd wanted that more than anything.

But Martina knew better than to put her momentary desires above her common sense. And her common sense told her being with him would lead to the inevitable pain of a breakup sooner or later. And doing it sooner would be less painful than doing it later, when he'd become so much a fixture in her life that she would not be able to imagine being without him.

What it came down to was that she didn't want the kind of life he represented. She didn't want to live in a huge house with so many cars in the garage that there were vehicles she'd never even seen. Hell, she hadn't known he had an SUV until he offered to drive everyone to the hospital in it. What kind of person lived like that?

She didn't want that, and she didn't want to live a life that became so much about the lifestyle, rather than the people living it, that the idea of having children who might put a crimp in that lifestyle was simply inconceivable.

She wanted love. She wanted a small house of her own that felt like a home. She wanted her sisters near her. And she wanted children.

Was that so much to ask?

For him it was, and that didn't seem like an obstacle that could be overcome.

She was glad the kitchen project was nearly done, because once it was, she'd have little reason to be around him anymore. They'd talked about more extensive remodeling, but there'd been no contract to that effect, so she was free to walk away.

As for the Hall property, it had gone up on the MLS the day before, and Martina had already put in an offer. If it was accepted, she would have to see Chris's name on the documents she'd be signing over the course of the thirty-day escrow. If it wasn't accepted —if someone else made a higher offer and beat her out for the property—then she'd have no reason to see him anymore at all.

Except that, despite everything, she ached for him. Her body yearned for him with a strength that felt like a desperate hunger, a life-threatening thirst. She didn't know if she was strong enough to resist him. But she had to try.

"It's crazy," Chris told Will a few days later when they were having lunch at a place in Morro Bay, eating hot dogs loaded with mustard, relish, pickles, and hot peppers. "Since when does a woman dump a man because he has too much money?" He knew he was simplifying things, but stating it that way helped him to tell Will about the sheer absurdity of it.

"I don't think that's why she did it." Will examined his hot dog studiously. The thing was too big to consume in normal bites, and he seemed to be contemplating a strategy.

"Well, that was part of it." Chris took a bite of his dog, chewed, and swallowed. He wiped a dribble of spicy mustard from his lips. "Then there was the baby thing." In fact, the baby thing had been the factor that had pushed things off the cliff, but he presented it as though it were a barely significant side issue.

"The baby thing," Will repeated.

"Yes. Well ... I might have indicated I wasn't eager to have children. And I might have done it while she was holding her newborn nephew." God, he really was an asshole. He was beginning to see that —though there was no reason Will should have to understand it just as clearly.

"I see." Will attempted a bite of his dog. He did this in a way that was much more civilized than most people attempted such a task— more civilized, in fact, than the way Chris himself had done it. That left Will relatively mustard-free as he ate. Interesting.

"It's possible the baby thing was a bigger deal than the money thing," Chris admitted. "With the money thing plus the baby thing ..." He left that thought out there.

"A cumulative effect," said Will, sounding like the professor he was.

"Yes."

"So, *did* you try to buy her?" Will asked, getting right to the point.

"Of course not. No!" Chris considered it. "Although ..."

"Although?"

"Although, I might have imagined she would be more interested in a serious relationship with me if I ... you know. If I greased the wheels a little on the thing with the property."

"So, yes, you were trying to buy her," Will concluded. "But there's another thing that interests me about what you just said."

Chris waited, trying not to let his irritation show.

"You said it might make her more interested in a serious relationship."

"So?" Chris asked.

"So, you just said you want a *serious* relationship. Serious. You don't just want to sleep with her or date her. You want it to be something long-term. Something real."

He really had said that, hadn't he? His first impulse was to deny that was what he'd meant, but when he dropped his defensiveness and really thought about it ... yes. He'd said it, and he'd meant it.

"Yeah." He nodded. "I'd like that."

"Okay, now we're getting somewhere. She was upset you don't want kids, so she's obviously on the same page about wanting something serious."

Now that Will was saying it that way, Chris felt unaccountably pleased. Which was odd, since he and Martina were no longer together.

"Okay." He waited for Will to continue.

"So," Will said, "the issue isn't what you want, it's what you did to try to get it."

"I can see that."

"Also." Will held up one finger as though he were lecturing a class and was about to introduce a particularly salient point. "There's the issue of how intractable you are on the child issue. You don't want children now, but do you think that might change? Is it an issue of timing, or are you dead set against reproducing?"

He'd never thought about it, really. He'd simply had an instantaneous, gut reaction to Martina's question about kids, and now he was experiencing the consequences.

"I haven't really considered it."

"Well," Will said in a way that suggested he was too polite to voice his opinion that Chris was acting like an idiot, "I think you should start considering it."

33

M artina's offer on the Hall property was accepted. She hoped Chris had kept his promise and had let his attorney handle things. He'd said he wouldn't know the identity of the person buying the property until the deal was being finalized, and she hoped that was true.

In any case, she was paying fair market value. She wasn't getting any kind of special treatment, so even if he did know she was the buyer, her conscience would be clear. This was going to be her property, her project. And eventually, she hoped, her home.

On the day she got the news, she brought a bottle of champagne home from the grocery store, determined to celebrate even though she didn't feel particularly festive.

She poured the wine for everyone at dinner that night—herself, Benny, Sofia, and Patrick. She'd invited Bianca and her family, but they were too busy with the baby.

"What's this for?" Benny asked.

"We're celebrating." Martina had made a nice dinner that night— vegetarian manicotti with a salad of organic vegetables she'd bought at the farmer's market.

"You and Chris got back together? Oh, thank God," Sofia said.

"No, we didn't." Martina's mood suddenly dampened at the sound of his name.

"Do you see him here?" Benny asked dryly. "I assume if we were celebrating their reconciliation, he'd be here for the party."

Patrick valiantly tried to get the conversation back on its original track. "What are we celebrating, Martina?"

"My offer on the Hall property was accepted. I'm going to buy a house."

They all raised their glasses and clinked them delicately before drinking.

"That's great, Martina," Patrick said. "I'm really happy for you."

"So am I," Sofia said. "But ... you're buying it from Chris, right? Isn't that going to be weird?"

"Hell, yes, it's weird," Benny said. "You know how many papers you're going to have to sign? And his name is going to be on every one of them, right under yours. Christopher X. Mills."

"His middle name doesn't start with X," Martina said, frowning. "Where did the X come from?"

"I thought it sounded ominous." Benny wiggled her fingers in a way that was supposed to indicate monsters, maybe, or crawling insects.

"Well. No, it's not weird," Martina lied. "We had a deal. He was going to put the property on the market, and his lawyer was going to decide which offer to accept without knowing anything about me. And that's what happened. I'm paying a fair price. I did not screw my way into this property. I am not a prostitute." Martina hadn't known that last part was going to come out, but now that it had, the others were staring at her in awkward silence.

"Okay, then," Patrick said.

"Martina. Did he say something to make you feel that way? Because, I've got to tell you, I've been itching to punch somebody in the face lately, just on general principles. I'd be happy to go over there. Two birds, one stone," Benny said.

"God. No! He did not say anything to make me feel that way."

Martina, frustrated, put down her glass. "Except, he kind of did. Because the whole way he tried to buy the place for me ..."

"I buy Sofia things all the time," Patrick said, not unreasonably. "I've never associated that with her ... ah ... providing services for payment."

"I know." Martina slugged down the rest of her champagne, no longer feeling festive but instead just wanting to stop feeling the way she was feeling. "I know it. But I'm not talking about rational facts. I'm taking about my feelings. I'm talking about emotions. I'm talking about how he took something good, something exciting—me wanting to buy my own place—and turned it into ... into ..." She grasped for words.

"Into whoring for land," Benny supplied.

"Well ... yes," Martina admitted. "And all of that might be something we could work through, but if he never wants children—if he thinks having kids with me would be worse than a stretch in a maximum-security prison—then I'm not sure it's worth trying to work it out."

Patrick cleared his throat. "Um ... May I say something?"

"Sure," Martina said.

"It's just ... I have a hard time thinking it's not worth fixing if you love him. If you love somebody, then it's worth any amount of effort. It's worth—"

"Nearly drowning?" Sofia suggested. Patrick had, in fact, nearly drowned in his first foolhardy attempt to woo Sofia. Fortunately, Sofia had rescued him. Which had, certainly, turned out to be worth her time and exertions.

"It's worth it if she loves him," Benny put in. "So, do you?"

"I don't know," Martina said.

She'd dated men, and she'd liked many of them. But she'd never been in love. What did it feel like? This gnawing, aching feeling she had when he wasn't around—was that love? The sense of being at peace when she was in his arms—was that love? That feeling that she wanted to know where he was and what he was doing all of the time, even when she wasn't anywhere nearby. Was that what love felt like?

If so, then yes, she loved him. But didn't love also mean being with him would enhance her life rather than upending it?

That last thought seemed profound to her, so she put it out there.

"Isn't love supposed to be easy? Isn't it supposed to feel good? If I'm in love, then why do I feel so awful?"

Benny guffawed. "That's the stupidest thing I've ever heard."

Martina was offended. "What? Why?"

"Love is brutal. Love sucks. Love will make you wish you were dead. Haven't you ever listened to a country-western song?"

"Then what's the point?" Martina threw her hands into the air in despair. "Why even try, then?"

"Because." Sofia took Patrick's hand. "If you can get through the wishing you were dead part, it's pretty great."

WHEN CHRIS GOT the news his attorney had accepted an offer on his behalf for the Hall property, he hoped like hell the offer had been Martina's. How much would it suck if he'd gone through all of this just for someone else to get the land?

He supposed he'd know for sure when it was time to sign the papers. Until then, it wasn't his concern anymore. He'd bought the property for her, but she didn't want it from him. So be it. Either she'd get it on her own terms, or she wouldn't.

It seemed the property on Lodge Hill was one of many things he wanted to give her that she didn't want to accept.

He was thinking about all of that as he stood in his garage looking at the parts of his car door, which were laid out on the floor on a drop cloth.

All of this time, all of this work, and he still hadn't managed to put the damned door back together. Why couldn't he do this? How hard could it be?

He could buy his way out of it, of course—he could hire someone to come over and do it for him. But he didn't want that. He wanted to do it himself. He wanted to put his own loving care into the car so when it was done, he would feel that sense of pride and satisfaction, that feeling that the car was really his.

Oh, shit.

That was exactly what Martina wanted from the Hall property, wasn't it?

She wanted precisely that—to do this on her own so she could feel satisfaction and ownership, so she could feel the pride of having created something of value.

He really hadn't seen that before. Why hadn't he? Why had he been so dense?

Seeing it now—having this revelation—made him so pleased with himself that he couldn't wait to tell Karen.

WHEN CHRIS SAW Karen the following week, she was impressed with his new insight into Martina's feelings, just as he'd expected her to be. But she was less impressed with him for failing to take action on it.

"Why are you telling me this and not Martina?" she asked.

He'd sat there staring at her like a five-year-old being told about molecular biology: no comprehension.

"But—"

"You've just unlocked one of the things keeping you apart, and that's great." Karen had carefully folded her hands in her lap, looking at him indulgently. "But it won't do you any good if Martina doesn't know about it."

OKAY, so he was a fool who had shockingly little in the way of natural instincts when it came to women—and interpersonal relationships in general. One could argue he shouldn't have to be told why the woman he loved—and, let's face it, he did love her—felt the way she did or why it was important. But *shouldn't* didn't have much to do with things.

He *did* need to be told. He *did* need to ruminate on things for a while before he understood why he'd said or done something offensive.

He also needed to ruminate a while before he knew what to do about it.

Now that Karen had kicked his ass on the subject of communication with Martina, he was finally on track to clear up one of the things that had been coming between them.

There was nothing he could do about the baby thing—at least, not yet, not until he figured out where he really stood on that—but at least he could clear up the issue of the Hall property.

He asked her to have coffee with him one morning at Jitters. At first she said no, she had too much work to do, and anyway, what would be the point? But he managed to persuade her, telling her he had something important to say to her.

Now, as he got ready for the coffee date, showering and shaving and applying a subtle amount of cologne, he was nervous about how it was going to go. He was showing up prepared to admit he'd been wrong, which was certainly a point in his favor. But it was only one piece of the puzzle. If she said, *That's great, Chris, but what about the babies,* he knew he'd be screwed. Because he didn't have an answer for her on that one yet.

He wasn't sure he ever would.

34

He showed up at Jitters early and staked out a table at the back of the room. He picked it carefully—something quiet, not too close to the bathrooms, away from the hiss of the milk steamer but close enough to the buzz of activity that Martina wouldn't feel like he was hiding her away.

He mentally rehearsed what he wanted to say, and when he saw her come in the front door of the coffee house, looking around the room for him, her coat slung over her arm, he felt buoyed.

Surely he could still rescue this thing between them.

"Chris." She came to him, a polite smile on her face.

"Can I order something for you?" He pulled out a chair for her and took her coat, lying it carefully over a spare chair.

She told him she wanted chamomile tea, so he went to the counter to order it. Getting her drink for her was not only the polite thing to do, it also gave him a little extra time to settle himself and prepare.

When he had the drink in his hand, he went back to the table, placed it in front of her, and sat down.

Of course, it didn't make sense to just launch into it without softening her up a little, so he started with small talk.

"How's Sofia's wedding coming along?"

"It's good." Martina nodded. "Everything's pretty much in place. Sofia was nervous before the bridal shower, but now she seems to have calmed down a bit."

"It's getting close," he said.

The nod again. "Less than two weeks."

There was a time when he'd assumed he would be Martina's date for the wedding, but now he supposed he would just hear about it after the fact. Too bad. He liked weddings. He liked cake. He would have liked to escort Martina, to dance with her and watch her sway to the music in her bridesmaid dress.

"If you need a place to hold it at the last minute because of a broken pipe, I'm your man," he joked.

He tried not to think too much about that last clause in the sentence, that *I'm your man*. Because he was, whether she wanted it to be true or not. He simply was.

"I'm really hoping that won't be necessary," she said. "But thank you. And thank you for what you did for us with the shower. If I didn't say it before—"

"You did."

"Well ... good. It really meant a lot. You saved us."

He liked the thought of having saved her, liked the image of himself as one of the action figures in the glass cases in his study. That's all he was trying to do when he'd bought the property, after all. He'd been trying to save the day. But now he could see Martina hadn't needed a hero. She'd needed someone to support her while she became the heroine of her own life. And that was an entirely different thing.

Martina sipped her tea. "So. What was it you wanted to talk to me about?"

He picked up his coffee cup, fidgeted with it a little, then put it carefully back down on the table. "I was working on my car the other day. The Mustang."

"How's that coming?" she asked.

"Fine. Well, actually, not fine at all. That's the point. I was in my garage looking at all of these parts lying on a tarp on the floor, and I was thinking about how I was never going to get them all put back where they belong. And I thought—and, Martina, this is the important part—I thought I could hire someone to do it for me. But I didn't want to do that. I wanted to do it myself so when it's done, I can have that satisfaction of knowing I put in the effort and created something on my own."

She listened silently as he went on.

"And I realized, that's what you wanted to do with the Hall property, and that's what I took away from you when I bought it and tried to give it to you. I see that now, and I'm sorry."

She averted her gaze, looking down at the tabletop instead of at him. Despite that, he could see he'd reached her. He could see that what he'd said meant something.

"Yes." She spoke softly. "That's exactly right."

He felt a surge of triumph, knowing he'd gotten it—he'd understood.

"Please tell me your offer was the one we accepted."

"It was." She did look at him now, smiling. "You mean you really didn't know?"

"I really didn't know. You asked me to stay out of it, and I did. I didn't even tell my attorney your name."

Her color changed—a hint of pink rising in her cheeks—and that fascinated him. He loved the way he could see her emotions on her face as easily as if he were reading a sign.

"So, congratulations," he went on. "I can't wait to see what you do with it." He just hoped she would let him in enough for him to be part of it.

"You really didn't get it before," she said, almost as though she were talking to herself, as though she were sorting it all out. "You really didn't see why I was upset about it."

"No, but I do now." Sometimes he was a little slow that way, but he got to the right place in the end. At least, he had this time.

～

MARTINA'S COFFEE with Chris was eye-opening. Until now, she'd thought he understood why she'd been upset about what he'd done —he just didn't agree or care. But now she could see he really hadn't gotten it. He'd genuinely thought he'd done something nice for her, and he'd been baffled when she'd been not only ungrateful but angry.

She still didn't think she'd been wrong in the way she'd reacted. But she began to soften toward him, knowing he'd been clueless rather than controlling.

The thing was, he was actively working to see her point of view. How often did people do that? In her experience, rarely. It made her optimistic about him and his potential.

She stayed at Jitters with him for a while, talking about her plans for the property, how the wedding was coming along, how her sisters were, and how her business was doing. Then they talked about him and his efforts to put back the parts of his car door.

"I didn't think it would be this hard when I started it." He shook his head mournfully.

"The hard things are always the best once you get them right."

She believed that in her soul, and she allowed herself to think that maybe—just possibly—that philosophy might have some relevance to their relationship.

"I DON'T KNOW," she told Sofia later that day when they were making place cards for the reception. "I'm kind of thinking I might give it another chance. With Chris, I mean."

Sofia put down the caligraphy pen she was holding and looked at her sister. "Really? Why? I mean ... that's great. But what changed your mind?"

Martina shrugged, looking at the card she was working on instead of at Sofia. "He gets it now. At least, he's trying to. He really understands about why I didn't want the property from him. The thing is, he had to really work hard to get it, but he put in the effort."

"Well, that's something." Sofia picked up her pen again and crafted a few perfect letters on the card. "Most of the time when guys don't understand us, they think it's our problem—we're irrational or emotional, or whatever. And so, obviously, whatever we're feeling is wrong. That's one thing about Patrick. Whenever we disagree, he at least allows for the possibility he might be the one who's screwing up. And if he is, he'll admit it."

"Patrick's really great," Martina said fondly.

"He is. I love him so much, Martina," Sofia said, the card forgotten again.

Martina wanted to be happy for Sofia—she really did—and she *was* happy. But another part of her felt a gnawing ache at hearing about her sister's romantic bliss. Because Martina wanted that, too. She wanted all of it—the romance, the love, the unlimited future full of possibility and promise.

The more she thought about that, the more she thought she wanted all of those things with Chris.

"Do you think it's a mistake?" she asked. "Getting back together with Chris? Because I miss him, Sofia. I really miss him."

"I don't know." Sofia looked thoughtful. "I'm predisposed in his favor because of what he did the day of my shower. He was awesome. But you have to think about your goals and what you want for your future. If he doesn't change his mind about kids, and you guys stay together long term, is that going to be okay? Or will it eat away at you? Because you don't want to go into it setting yourself up for anger, resentment, and disappointment. It's not fair to you, and it's not fair to him, either." It was more of a speech than Sofia usually made, but Martina thought her points were solid.

"Maybe," Martina said after a while.

"Maybe to which part?"

"Maybe it would be okay if he doesn't change his mind about kids." Just saying that made Martina feel sick inside, made her feel heat behind her eyes, as though she might burst into tears. But the fact that she'd said it at all meant something significant. At least part of her was thinking that being with Chris would be worth giving up children for. And that was a major shift in her world.

"Seriously?" Sofia's eyes widened. "Do you mean that?"

"Maybe," Martina said again.

"You're more serious about him than I thought, then."

Martina was more serious about him than *she'd* thought, too.

She didn't want to give up anything. She didn't want to let go of the idea of one day being a mother. But she also didn't want this pain anymore, this ache of wanting him but not being able to have him.

She didn't know if she could keep living with the ache—not if she didn't have to.

First, when she and Chris had been seeing each other, Martina had planned to take him to the wedding as her date. Then, when they'd broken up, she'd told Sofia that he wouldn't be coming. Now, she'd changed her mind again.

"Um ... Sofia? About the guest list." It was just one week until the wedding, and the place cards were done. The RSVPs had come in. The caterers had been given the final head count.

"Oh, God. What? Which relative changed their mind at the last minute? Who wants to bring their second cousin's friend's babysitter? Because, I swear to God—"

"It's not that."

Of course it made sense Sofia had assumed such a scenario, because they'd been dealing with those kinds of requests for weeks.

"Then what?" Sofia asked.

"It's just ... I wondered if maybe ..."

"Spit it out, woman. The sooner you tell me who RSVP'd at the last freaking minute, the sooner I can tell you to kiss my—"

"It's Chris. I want to bring Chris."

Sofia stopped in midrant. "Oh. Really." She elongated that last word, giving it an inflection that suggested she was interested not for the sake of the head count, but for the pure, delicious interest of the thing.

"Well, I haven't asked him yet, but ... I want to. If you say it's okay, I'm going to." Martina was bolstering her own resolve even as she said it. "But if it's really a problem ..."

"No. No, no. Ask him." Sofia grinned.

"Are you sure? Because—"

"Ask him."

"But the caterers—"

"There's no problem with the caterers," Sofia said. "I already included him in the head count. I made a place card. I knew you'd change your mind and want him to come."

35

Martina asked Chris to be her wedding date, and of course, he said yes. She'd been nervous about asking him, but in retrospect, she wasn't sure why. He'd accepted her invitation as naturally as if he'd always known he was meant to do just that. Which he probably had.

The final week leading up to the wedding was a blur of last-minute arrangements, inquiries from out-of-town guests, efforts to soothe Sofia's nerves, and, for Martina, real estate paperwork. She also had a job to do, so she managed everything in between meetings with clients, work on the various designs she had in progress, and checking in with Noah and his crew.

By the evening of Sofia's bachelorette party, the night before the wedding, Martina couldn't wait to get her sister married so she could move on with her life.

Also, she couldn't wait for the wedding so she could see Chris again.

~

THE BACHELORETTE PARTY was held at Ted's, a bar well away from

Main Street where the locals went to drink and get away from the steady flow of tourists. The place was a dive, but a comfortable, friendly dive, with a jukebox, a couple of pool tables, a dart board, and lighting so dim you could barely see the stains on the ancient, tamped-down carpet.

They'd discussed going somewhere more upscale for the party— one of the Paso Robles wineries, maybe—but that hadn't been in their mother's wedding plan. Carmela had insisted the bachelorette party should be somewhere close to home to make it easy for everyone to get back where they belonged after a night of carousing.

The plan also called, sensibly, for a designated driver. Bianca had volunteered to do it because she couldn't drink much while nursing the baby, but that wouldn't work, because she also couldn't stay out late while the baby was at home waiting to be fed. So, Martina stepped in. She'd never enjoyed drinking as much as other people did, so she was the logical choice.

They all met at nine p.m.: ten women, including the four sisters; a nurse and a physician's assistant from Bianca's medical office, where Sofia worked; a couple of Sofia's friends from various places, including the gym where she worked out; Patrick's sister, Fiona; and Lucy Alba, the wife of Patrick's best friend, Ramon.

The bar wasn't really set up for a large group, so they pulled two round tables as close together as they could and put five chairs around each one. They ordered pitchers of beer and shots of tequila —and an iced tea for Martina. Ted, the bar's owner, scowled at the women as he brought their drinks.

"Bachelorette party," the man muttered, as though the very words hurt his face. "You'd better not have any strippers coming in here."

"No strippers," Martina reassured him.

"Really?" Sofia's face fell. "I thought there would be strippers."

The two women from Bianca's medical office went to the pool tables, and Lucy and one of Sofia's gym friends followed them, hoping to get in on the next game. Martina challenged Sofia to a game of darts, and Bianca and Benny went along to heckle.

"Ten dollars?" Martina asked as they gathered the darts.

"Ten? I don't have ten dollars. I've just paid for a wedding."

"Five, then," Martina said.

"Hello, wedding bills! Those little Jordan almonds aren't free," Sofia protested.

Martina put a hand on her hip. "Okay. How about if I lose, I pay you ten dollars, and if you lose, you have to do the Chicken Dance at the reception."

Sofia considered the proposal. "That's fair. You want to go first?"

The dart board was so riddled with holes from previous players that it seemed like there was little to hold it together. Still, Martina took her place behind the line of masking tape on the floor and lined up her shot. She threw the first dart, and it missed the board entirely, sticking into the wall next to it.

"Ha! No Chicken Dance for me," Sofia said, hooting in glee.

"I'm just getting warmed up." Martina took another shot and did better this time. The dart was still way off center, but it landed on the board for three points.

Martina finished her turn—her score was dismal—and Sofia took hers. While they played, the conversation went to Chris. It wasn't random, Martina decided. Her sisters had been angling to bring it up.

"So, I put you and Chris at the table closest to the cake," Bianca said mildly, grinning as though the near-the-cake placement were a big favor. "You'll get first dibs, after the bride and groom."

"It's going to be really good cake," Benny offered. "Of course, all cake is good cake."

"Except the one you made last year for Bianca's birthday," Sofia reminded her.

Benny looked thoughtful. "True. I don't think lemon cake is supposed to be that color."

"It was still thoughtful, though," Bianca said.

"So, anyway." Sofia brought the topic back to where it had started. "You'll get the cake first. Whether it's the right color or not."

"I'm sure it will be," Martina said.

They finished the first game, and Sofia won. Martina fished a ten out of her purse and gave it to her sister, who held it over her head and waved it around, doing a little victory dance.

Benny and Bianca were up, and Martina and Sofia moved to the side to watch.

"So, Chris," Bianca said, her laserlike attention to the topic unaffected by alcohol, since she'd only had half a beer. "What did he say when you invited him?"

"He said yes." Martina kept her tone neutral. "I mentioned that. That's why he's sitting with me near the cake."

"Yes, but how did he say it? Was he excited?" Bianca took a shot, and her dart came dangerously close to the bull's eye.

"Jeez. I didn't know you were good at darts," Martina said.

"Back on topic." Bianca paused before her second throw. "Where do things stand between you two?"

Martina sighed, knowing she wouldn't be able to avoid answering the question.

"I don't know. I mean, yes, he seemed excited. Or at least happy. Very happy. He seemed like he was really glad I asked him. But as for where we stand? Who knows? I want to be with him. I really do. And the kids thing ... oh, man." She was starting to get teary-eyed, so she stopped talking long enough to dab at her eyes with a bar napkin.

Benny put a hand on Martina's arm as she got herself together.

"The kids thing," Martina tried again, "is hard. But people give up things for the people they love all the time. It's what we do."

"The 'people we love'," Bianca said softly. "So, you love him."

"Yeah." Martina let in a shaky breath. "I do."

Sofia said, "Loving somebody, though ... You have to be careful that what you give up is something you can live with. Loving him isn't enough if, ten years from now, when you're in perimenopause and your eggs are drying up, you can't stop resenting him because you don't have children, and you won't have grandchildren, and there'll be nobody to take care of you in your old age."

It wasn't as though Martina hadn't thought of that herself. But hearing Sofia lay it out like that made it seem like a stark and frightening possibility.

"I can be seething with resentment in ten years, or I can be miserable right now," Martina said. "And I *am* miserable without him. I am. So, if it's a question of pain now or pain later ..."

"Maybe there shouldn't be any pain at all," Benny said. "Or, at least, maybe there shouldn't be such a strong possibility of it."

Martina let in a shaky breath. "Ah, jeez. That's enough of this. Can we just play darts?"

THE DAY OF THE WEDDING, unlike the day of the bridal shower, dawned bright and crisp. They had all stayed at the bar until after one a.m., and Sofia and Benny were moaning with their hangovers as they moved around the kitchen to get their morning fix of caffeine.

Martina wasn't hungover, having had nothing but glass after glass of either iced tea or water. But she'd been up late driving people to their homes or hotels, so she felt groggy from lack of sleep. Usually, she was a tea person in the morning, but today, she opted for strong coffee. It had been a long night, and it was promising to be an even longer day.

"Yikes." Benny looked at Sofia over their steaming mugs of coffee. "You should see the circles under your eyes. You look like a raccoon that lost a boxing match."

"Thank you." Sofia glared at her sister. "That's exactly what I need to hear on the morning of my wedding, when it's critically important I look more beautiful than I ever have."

"Don't worry," Martina said soothingly. "The makeup artist will be able to cover that right up. You'll look poreless and perfect."

In truth, Sofia always looked poreless and perfect to Martina. She did look a bit tired and hungover this morning, but she was still lovely. Martina had spent most of her teen years resenting that Sofia was prettier than she was—the prettiest, in fact, of all of the Russo sisters—and she no doubt would have outshone all of them today even if she hadn't had the benefit of being the bride.

"Have you called Patrick yet?" Martina asked, trying to get off the subject of Sofia's looks.

"Yeah." Sofia grinned. "He's nervous, but he said a lot of really sweet things about our life together that made me want to do fun, naked things to him."

Patrick was staying at Bianca and TJ's house because Sofia didn't want him to see her today until the big reveal at the church. With luck, he wouldn't even be aware of her dark circles.

"He's one of the good ones," Martina said.

"I know. I can't wait to marry him. Oh! And we're going to start trying to have kids right away. Tonight, probably." Sofia saw the look on Martina's face and gasped in alarm. "Oh, no. I'm sorry, Martina. I didn't mean—"

"It's fine."

"No, it's not. I didn't—"

"Sofia." Martina took her sister's hand. "You're allowed to be happy. And whatever may or may not be going on between me and Chris shouldn't change that. I'm fine. It's wonderful you're going to start trying. I mean that." She leaned over and hugged Sofia tightly.

"Yeah, yeah," Benny said. She looked more tired than Sofia did, though it seemed unkind to point that out. "I'd rather not think about her and Patrick 'trying,' if you don't mind. I'm already nauseous."

36

Chris was looking forward to the wedding. For one thing, he liked Sofia, and he liked Patrick, too. He genuinely wished them well, and it was going to be good to see someone get the romantic happy ending they deserved.

Second, it was going to give him a chance to dress up, which he rarely did these days. He had a couple of excellent suits in his closet, and it would be nice to get one out and put it to use.

And third, it would be nice to see Martina.

Oh, hell. Who was he kidding? Seeing Martina wasn't third. It was first, second, and last. It was everything. It was all that mattered.

On the morning of the wedding, he laid out his clothes, thinking not only about the ceremony and the reception but about how he could get Martina to go all in with him.

Yes, the fact that she'd invited him meant something—meant, certainly, she was softening in her resolve to be finished with him. But he didn't just want her to tentatively spend time with him. He wanted her to give things another full-out try; he wanted her to enthusiastically throw herself into their relationship.

And he wanted to find a way to let himself do the same.

Obviously, his statement that he never wanted kids had been an effort to distance himself from her, to keep himself safe from the vulnerability of a real, meaningful relationship.

Okay, so maybe it wasn't that obvious. Maybe he'd needed Karen to tell him. But still.

Why did you say that, Chris? Karen had asked him. *Did you mean it? Do you really object to the idea of ever having children?*

At first, he'd assured her he had meant it—he did really object to the idea of himself ever procreating. But the more they'd talked, the more he'd started to question his motives.

Ask yourself what this has to do with your own parents, she'd said.

The irritating thing about therapy was that she wouldn't just outright tell him what it had to do with his own parents. Instead, she'd assigned him to think about it.

So he had.

But the more he thought about it, the more the answers eluded him. His mother was a drunk. His father had left—and had only returned to ask for money. They hadn't shaped him; he'd had to shape himself. So what relevance could the two of them possibly have to his current love life?

Ask yourself what this has to do with your own parents.

It was like a puzzle with several key pieces missing. Or like the parts of a car door. The harder he tried to put everything together, the bigger the mess he made.

He ruminated over the whole thing while he showered, while he drank his second cup of coffee of the day, while he sat in his study and browsed his social media, and while he paced restlessly through the cavernous spaces of his house.

Ask yourself what this has to do with your own parents.

Frustrated, he called Karen on her cell phone.

"It doesn't have anything to do with my own parents," he said when she picked up. "How could it? They're barely in my life."

"Chris, this number is for emergencies. Are you having a mental health emergency right now?" Her voice was calm and even.

He hesitated. "In a manner of speaking, yes."

"Are you a danger to yourself or others?"

"I'm in danger of ruining this thing with Martina if I can't figure out what my problem is. So, yes. Yes, I am. I'm a danger to my own relationship."

"That's not what I meant, and I think you know that." Her voice was as serene as a mountain lake.

"Look. I'm going to see her again today. She invited me to her sister's wedding. This is big, and I don't want to fuck it up. So, a little help, here?"

Karen let out a gentle sigh. "I would suggest to you, Chris, that your troubles with Martina have more to do with your relationship to your own parents than you're willing to admit."

He rubbed his forehead with his free hand. "Yes, you've made that clear. I just don't think—"

"Why are you dismissing it?"

"Because they're barely in my life!" He was raising his voice now, and he had to make an effort to modulate his tone.

"Don't you think that's something to examine?"

"What is?"

"They're barely in your life, and when they are, they represent something burdensome to you."

He was about to throw his phone at the wall. "So?"

"So, might that not color the way you think about having children? Might that not color the way you view the experience of being a child?"

"That's ... I don't ..."

"We'll talk about it more at your next session, Chris. Enjoy the wedding." And then she was gone.

MARTINA AND CHRIS had agreed to meet at the wedding. He'd wanted to pick her up, but Martina would be going to the church early to help Sofia get ready, pose for the bridal party photos, and generally run interference should any last-minute problems come up. Unless he wanted to be at the church three hours before the ceremony, it made more sense for him to meet her there.

Once Sofia, Benny, and Martina arrived at the church, each of them with voluminous dresses in garment bags thrown over their arms, Martina was glad he wasn't here. The whole thing was barely controlled chaos, and she wanted to have herself together—both in terms of her appearance and her emotions—when she saw him.

Right now, all three of them were a mess of sweatpants, hair scrunchies, flip-flops, and facial blemishes, and they wouldn't be ready for male eyes until they'd changed clothes and the hairdresser and makeup artist had finished with them.

Bianca was already at the church when they got there. "There you are! Oh. Jeez. We shouldn't have had the bachelorette party the night before the wedding. You look like Keith Richards after a bad bout of insomnia."

"Which one of us?" Sofia asked.

"All of you."

"Look who's talking," Benny barked back at her. "You look like you haven't slept in weeks."

"I haven't," Bianca said. "But I have a newborn, so I have a good excuse."

"Oh, God," Sofia moaned. "I need to be beautiful for my wedding. Tell me I'm going to be beautiful for my wedding."

"You will be," Martina said soothingly. "The makeup artist is going to make you look as fresh as an alpine meadow."

The baby was asleep in his carrier as they got settled in the bride's room. Martina, Benny, and Sofia took turns oohing and aahing at him —quietly, to avoid waking him—as Bianca fussed with the contents of her diaper bag.

"TJ's going to be on call—he'll be able to swoop in and take AJ at a moment's notice if he starts to fuss. We just thought it would be easier for him to start the day here with me so I can feed him. I hope that's okay, Sofia. I know it's your day, and I didn't want—"

"It's perfect. I love having him here." Sofia was beaming, the effects of her hangover starting to wane in favor of the excitement of being a bride. "God, he's perfect. Isn't he?"

"He is." Bianca looked lovingly down at her son. "Though, he's a little less perfect when he wakes up at three a.m. with a raging attitude and a full diaper."

"Knock knock!"

They all looked toward the door, where a woman with armloads of photography equipment was leaning in and greeting them.

"Oh." The woman frowned. "Maybe we should start with the dress and the rings until the hair and makeup people get here."

37

C hris sat in the pew he'd been shown to by one of the ushers. The church was Catholic, which made sense, given Sofia's Italian ancestry. A string quartet played some undefinable, soft music as the guests found their seats. Jesus, on the cross, looked down on Chris sternly.

On this side of the church were mostly people with dark hair and Mediterranean coloring. On the other, the assembled guests were mostly fair of skin and hair, with more than a few of them looking like they might be prone to melanoma if they didn't keep up their sunscreen regimen.

He felt somewhat uncomfortable, though he couldn't say why. A few rows ahead of him, Bianca's husband, TJ, cradled their baby in his arms, looking at the boy with undisguised love. He was cooing something to the baby, jiggling him in his arms.

Ten minutes before the ceremony was scheduled to begin, Bianca came down the aisle in her bridesmaid dress to check on her son. Finding him well cared for and content, she hurried back up the aisle to attend to her duties.

At the appointed time, when the clock indicated it was precisely two p.m., the men assembled at the altar: Patrick; his best man, a guy named Ramon whom Chris had met once or twice; a man who looked so much like Patrick it had to be his brother; and another man Chris had never met but who had the studious look of a college professor—no doubt one of Patrick's friends from the university. Chris supposed TJ would be up there, as well, if he hadn't had responsibility for the baby.

The music changed, and the procession began. The ring bearer. The flower girl. And then the bridesmaids, one by one.

First was Bianca, who was trying to keep her eyes forward but whose attention kept drifting to her husband and son. Then Benny, looking surprisingly at home in a long, floaty dress.

And then, there was Martina.

Chris was transfixed.

Did people say bridesmaid dresses were ugly? Were they considered to be less than optimal for showcasing a woman's beauty? Martina looked like a goddess, like some kind of forest nymph, in a dress the color of pink champagne or perhaps a woman's blush. Her glorious hair hung down her back in auburn waves, and she wore a wreath of flowers on her head. Her shoulders, all creamy, flawless skin and sinuous form, were bare. The neckline of the dress plunged into a deep V, giving him a glimpse of the perfect, soft curves of her breasts.

Had there ever been a woman so beautiful? Had there ever been anyone more perfect?

Everyone stood as the music changed to Wagner's "Bridal Chorus," but Chris didn't notice until he was the last one still seated. He couldn't focus on anyone—or anything—but Martina.

As Sofia walked up the aisle alone, holding her bouquet, she looked beautiful. Striking. She would have been perfectly at home on the cover of a magazine. But, God, Chris felt as though the very molecules of air and light in the room converged around Martina. The energy circled her, as though the space around her was where everything good lived. Everything hopeful.

When she turned to face the altar, the halter back of her dress showed an expanse of silky skin.

He couldn't say exactly what was happening to him. He'd been struck stupid by the sight of her. He'd seen Martina looking beautiful before. He'd seen her naked, when she'd been perhaps the most beautiful of all. But seeing her walking down an aisle in a church to the music of a string quartet, in the sight of God and an assembly of well-wishers? Well, that was something he'd been entirely unprepared for.

How big of a cliché was he, only realizing the power of his love for Martina in the context of a wedding? This was why people didn't invite casual dates to weddings, he supposed. At least, he never had.

When he tore his gaze away from Martina to look at the others standing at the altar, he noticed Patrick. The man was looking at Sofia with utter devotion, his eyes red as he brushed away a tear that glimmered on his cheek.

He looked the way Chris felt.

Maybe it had been a mistake to come. Chris felt his life choices narrowing even as he sat here. He felt as though his destiny were being formed and shaped without his consent right in front of him.

ONCE THE WEDDING WAS OVER, pictures had to be taken. Everyone had to be ushered to the reception venue and entertained until the bride and groom arrived. The priest and the quartet had to be paid, and the women had to clean all of their things out of the room they'd used to get ready.

Martina, Benny, and Bianca focused on attending to business so Sofia could simply bask in her role as the bride.

The photographer had taken a lot of the formal photos outside, where the temperature was barely in the fifties, so by the time they had their things loaded into the limo and were on their way to the reception, Martina could barely feel her fingers and toes, and she shivered as they blasted heat into the back of the car.

Sofia and Patrick, who would be posing for a slew of photos on their own now that the ones with the wedding party were finished, would be coming in a separate car.

Martina, Benny, Bianca, TJ, and AJ basked in the comfort of the limousine as they headed toward the winery in Paso Robles where the reception would be held.

"Woo! That's done. Give me the champagne." Benny reached out while Martina handed her the bottle the driver had provided to them.

She uncorked the bottle with a loud pop that made AJ cry.

"Aww, sweetie." Bianca soothed the baby, who was buckled into his car seat. "Mommy needs a drink. Just a little one. Okay? Just a little one." She cooed the last words in a baby-friendly tone that made the sounds almost undistinguishable as words.

Benny poured and handed around glasses of champagne—just a half glass for Bianca so it wouldn't interfere with her nursing. Since the rest of them had no such issues, Benny filled their glasses to the top.

"We did it. We finally got them married," Martina said with a happy sigh.

"Hallelujah." Benny took a deep drink of her champagne. "It was touch and go there for a while."

"Dad should have been here to walk her down the aisle." Bianca's face was pink, and she sniffled a little.

"Don't cry," Benny scolded her. "Then we'll all start, and it'll mess up our mascara. That makeup artist wasn't cheap."

"Worth every penny, though," Martina said. "We woke up this morning looking like the wrong half of *The Walking Dead*."

"Well, you all look beautiful now." TJ raised his glass to them.

"You had to say that," Benny said.

"Yes, I did," TJ agreed. "But it's still true."

As they rode through the rolling green hills along Highway 46 toward Paso Robles, with the blue Pacific Ocean stretched out in the distance far below them, Martina grew quiet. She'd seen how Chris had looked at her. She'd read his expression, and it had scared the hell out of her.

He was in this, she could see that. He was in it for the long term, if she wanted him. And she wasn't sure she'd have the strength to turn him away.

She looked at AJ, now sleeping soundly in his car seat, his lips pursed into a tiny rosebud as he made little murmuring sounds in his sleep.

She wanted a baby of her own someday with a longing that threatened to consume her.

But she was pretty sure she wanted Chris even more.

Tears threatened to come, and she blinked to force them back.

"You're thinking about Dad," Benny guessed. "Don't do that, I'm telling you. Remember your makeup."

Martina nodded. "Right." She didn't correct her sister.

THE RECEPTION WAS HELD in a big ballroom with windows over-looking the vineyards. The weather was glorious—bright sun and blue skies, even if the temperatures were a little cool. The band was already playing when they arrived, and the cake had been set up in one corner of the room. Round tables covered in white linen dotted the room, each with a centerpiece of pink and white roses.

Guests milled about with drinks in their hands, and tuxedoed waiters passed around trays of hors d'oeuvres.

Martina looked around the room until she found Chris, who was gazing at her with the same stark adoration she'd seen earlier. She went to him, took both of his hands in hers, and kissed him.

"Did you enjoy the wedding?" she asked.

"It was ... quite something," he said. "You look stunning."

She knew he wasn't just saying that. She knew, from the look on his face and the tone of his voice, that he meant every word.

"I have to say hi to everyone. Come on. I'll introduce you." She took him by the hand and went to greet aunts, uncles, cousins, friends, and acquaintances.

THE THING that struck Chris about meeting Martina's friends and relatives was that nobody recognized him, and nobody's eyes widened when they met him.

In the world he used to live in, up in Silicon Valley, he was known for his wealth and success, and every new acquaintance reacted to that—sometimes subtly, sometimes not. In that world, he was Christopher Mills, he was never just Chris.

This was different. Martina's relatives didn't know his name or his net worth, and more than that, they clearly didn't care. Instead, he was just Martina's new boyfriend, and that was how they evaluated him—based on whether the two of them seemed good together.

It was a welcome surprise. He couldn't remember the last time he'd been just another guy. He liked it.

"So, you're seeing our Martina, are you?" An older man with a comb-over and a course sprinkling of facial hair grabbed Chris's arm in a friendly squeeze. "Take care of her. She's special."

"I know she is," he told the man in all sincerity. "Believe me, I know it."

DINNER WAS SERVED, drinks were consumed, toasts were given. Then came the speeches.

The best man, Ramon, talked about his role in helping Patrick woo Sofia, a story that got some appreciative chuckles from the assembled group. Martina, who'd filled in as maid of honor due to Bianca's recent motherhood, said a few words about how happy she was for her sister and about what a wonderful man Patrick was.

Then, when they all thought the speeches were finished for the evening, Sofia stood and reached for the microphone.

After a brief introduction in which she spoke about her happiness and her love for Patrick, she began to speak about their father.

Oh, God, Martina thought. *I'm never going to make it through this.* She steeled herself and listened.

∽

CHRIS HAD BEEN HAVING a good time—certainly, a better time than he'd anticipated.

He'd enjoyed meeting everyone, and now he was feeling loose and comfortable after having a couple of glasses of champagne.

But under that lay a current of discomfort, one he couldn't quite put his finger on.

For one thing, it was the kids.

There were so many kids, ranging in age from Bianca's son to toddlers and awkward preteens, teenagers on the cusp of adulthood.

He didn't dislike kids, despite all that had been said between him and Martina about his reluctance to have any. He thought kids were fine, as long as someone else was raising them.

But seeing them here today, in such numbers, was unsettling.

There was AJ, being cuddled and held by his adoring father.

There was a very cute little girl, probably about three years old, who had been dancing with her father by standing on his feet, both of them grinning happily.

There was the little boy at the table across from them who was being lovingly cared for by his mother as she cut his meal into tiny chunks and gently encouraged him to try some foods he was unfamiliar with.

All of it added up to something he couldn't quite place. Some ache, some unnamed gnawing in his chest.

And that was why he didn't want kids, wasn't it? He didn't want to feel that gnawing, that phantom injury, all the time.

Who would?

Underneath it, he kept hearing Karen's voice in his head.

Don't you think your own childhood might be relevant here?

Isn't your own past something you should think about?

He had it under control, had the feelings firmly in check, until Sofia's speech.

Goddamn it, the speech.

∽

MARTINA BRACED herself as Sofia began to speak about Aldo, their father.

"You probably noticed no one walked me down the aisle today," Sofia said. "I had no shortage of volunteers. Patrick's father offered to do the honors, and I would have, indeed, been honored. My brother-in-law, TJ, stepped up, too, and I love him for that and for so many other things. I didn't turn down those offers due to lack of love or gratitude. I turned them down because I wasn't really alone. My father was beside me. I felt him there as surely as if he were still with us."

Martina muttered, "Damn it," and reached for a napkin to dab her eyes.

"My father—and my mother, too—meant so much to me and my sisters. They still do," Sofia went on. "They always will. He was at my side as I walked to Patrick. And she was with me when I said 'I do.' They'll both be with me every day of my life, with their love and encouragement. I'll always ..." Sofia's voice broke, and she took in a deep, shaky breath, tears falling down her cheeks. "I'll always look to their guidance in our marriage, because they showed me how to love. They showed me what a true partnership looks like. They taught me how to give myself to someone the way I gave myself to Patrick today, the way I hope to give myself to him every day. And they will be in my heart always. Mom, Dad, I love you." Sofia sat back down and dissolved into tears, and Patrick held her.

All three of them—Martina, Benny, and Bianca—were in various stages of recovery, wiping their eyes, heaving in shuddering breaths, reaching to take each other's hands.

Abruptly, Chris stood and stormed out of the room.

"What's that about?" TJ asked.

Martina looked after Chris as he left, and she saw the angry scowl on his face.

"I don't know. I just ... I don't know."

∾

SHE FOUND him outside in the vineyard, amid vines coming alive with tiny green buds. He had his back to her, his hands on his hips, looking down at the fertile earth.

Martina came up behind him, and he didn't look at her.

"Chris? What's wrong?"

He didn't say anything, so she tried again.

"Chris?"

He looked over his shoulder at her. "Why did you bring me here?" His voice simmered with barely restrained anger.

"What?"

"What exactly were you trying to accomplish with ..." He spread his arms. "All this?"

She kept her voice low, even. "I wasn't trying to accomplish anything. I just thought—"

"You thought what?" He spun around to face her. "What, Martina? You thought you could bring me here with your family, and your friends, and Sofia and Patrick, and the kids ..." He laughed bitterly. "All those kids. And you thought what? You could make me love you? Well, that part worked. I do. I do love you, God help me."

"Chris ..." She reached out to touch him, and he shook off her hand.

"Don't you get it?" he barked out at her.

"Get what?"

"I can never be what you need. Never. Martina ... Jesus. You deserve so much, but I can't give it to you. And you don't want what I do have to give. The property—"

"I thought we were past that."

"Yeah, well ... we're not." He looked bewildered, and she waited for him to go on. "Because if you're not interested in the money, there's nothing else I have that's worth giving."

Did he really think that? Was that really what he believed?

"That's not true."

"Isn't it? Alexis was only interested in what I could buy for her. My father..." He rubbed his face with his hands. "My father left and only contacted me when I had money to give him. I wasn't enough to keep my mother sober."

A fat tear ran down her cheek, but she said nothing—she just waited for him.

"I have never been enough for anyone in my life. Not one person. How can I possibly hope to be enough for a baby? For a child? For you?"

And there it was—the thing she hadn't understood, the thing that was holding him back from giving himself to her.

"You are enough." Her voice was barely above a whisper.

"No. No." He shook his head. "The way Sofia feels about your mother and father ... the way all of those kids in there today were laughing with their parents, having fun, just feeling safe and happy ... How can I give that to a child when I've never had it myself? When I don't even know what that looks like? It's impossible, Martina. I would fail you. And I don't want that to happen."

She could see his hands shaking. She wanted to go to him, to take him into her arms, but she sensed he wasn't ready yet. If she did that now, he'd push her away.

"What happened when you were a child was your parents' failure. Not yours. It was never yours."

He glanced at her, then looked back down at the ground, at the earth beneath his feet. "How do I know that? How can I believe that?"

Whether he was ready or not, she couldn't keep her distance anymore. She went to him and put her arms around him, and he held her, pressing his face into her bare shoulder.

"I'll believe it enough for both of us," she said.

38

S he went home with him that night, and she made love to him like a woman who'd waited decades just for the man in her arms. She gave herself to him wholeheartedly, cherishing his soul and his body.

Afterward, as she lay tucked up beside him, she tested the waters, feeling her way toward talking about everything that had happened.

"Chris?" She lay with her head on his chest, her arm across his belly. "What brought everything up for you? Why today?"

He stroked her hair languidly. "Weddings are about families. I guess it was just too much family in one day. Too much of all of those happy families."

"Because yours wasn't."

"No. It wasn't." He hesitated. "It's not that I don't want other people to be happy...."

"Of course not."

"It's just ... Why not me, you know? Why do other people get to have all of that, and I don't? Plus ..."

She raised up onto her elbow to look at him. "Plus what?"

"Plus, I've been talking to a therapist. Karen."

"You have?"

"Yeah. And some of the things she said ... I don't know. I was just thinking about them, that's all."

She positioned herself on top of him so she could be as close to him as possible. "Have you ever done that before? Seen a therapist?"

"No."

"So, why now?"

A wry grin pulled at his lips. "Well. I just thought ... it kind of matters more now. Me getting my shit together."

"Because of me?" Her heart sped up, and she felt a warm glow rise in her chest.

"Yes. Because of you." He carefully placed a kiss on the tip of her nose. "My relationships always fail. Always. And I don't want this one to fail."

"I don't either." She wiggled to get higher on his chest so she could kiss him. The kiss was long and delicious, and it made her feel as though she were in the perfect place—exactly where she belonged.

After a while, she said the thing she'd been gearing up to say. "Chris ... I don't need to have kids. Not really."

"I think you do. I think it's important to you, and you shouldn't have to give that up."

"Still ... I didn't mean right away. I didn't mean tomorrow. I—"

"I know. I get that." He brushed a lock of hair out of her face with one finger. "But someday. It's going to be important to you someday."

And someday soon, she thought. Her biological clock wasn't going to wait forever. But she didn't say that, because she really was willing to give it up for him. She could deal with the disappointment, if it came to that. As long as she had him.

"It's important. But it's not everything." But she could feel a swell of emotion—of sorrow—spreading through her at the thought.

"I've been thinking," he said. "I tried to give you something before that you didn't want, when I bought the property. Now, there's something you really do want that I can give you. Kids. Someday."

She could hear that it was hard for him to say. Hard for him to do, to offer her this.

"Are you saying ..."

"I'm saying, I'm working on it. And I'll keep working on it. I'm saying I'm not there yet, but I think I can get there."

"Really?" She tried to keep the happy squeal out of her voice, though she wasn't entirely successful.

"I could have another chance, right?" He gave her a lazy half grin. "I mean, my first parent-child relationship didn't go well, when I was the child. But this could be a chance to do it over. To do it right. With me on the other side of the equation."

"With me," she said.

"With you. Always with you."

He rolled her over so that he lay top of her, and after that, they didn't talk anymore.

THE NEXT DAY, they went to Martina's house, where everyone was getting together for breakfast for one last celebration before Sofia and Patrick left on their honeymoon.

Martina brought a box of pastries from the French Corner Bakery, and Benny was in the kitchen frying bacon. Bianca and TJ had just arrived with the baby, and Bianca was washing her hands at the kitchen sink so she could jump in to make her famous mushroom and mozzarella omelets.

Martina and Chris came in smiling, relaxed, and holding hands. That earned them some significant looks from the other Russos.

"Good morning, you two," Benny said from where she stood in front of a cast iron frying pan. "Looks like you had a good night."

"Not as good as Sofia and Patrick, probably," Martina said, deflecting attention from herself. "Are they even up yet?"

"Nope." Bianca started taking omelet ingredients out of the refrigerator. "Haven't heard a peep from them yet."

"Aww. That's sweet." Martina grinned. "They're going to have to get up if they want to have a leisurely breakfast and then get to the airport on time."

"Hey, newlyweds!" Benny called out. "Untangle from each other and get the hell up!"

A muffled, barely decipherable sound of protest came from Sofia and Patrick's bedroom.

"I brought bear claws!" Martina called out.

That did it. A few minutes later, Sofia came out in a bathrobe, her hair mussed and a smug smile on her face.

"Aw, jeez. Get a load of her," Benny said. "You'd think she and Patrick never did it before."

"We never did it as a married couple before. It's different. Better." She wiggled her eyebrows.

"Where's Patrick?" Chris asked.

"Taking a shower," Sofia said. "I'd have gotten in there with him, but there are bear claws."

∼

THEY ALL ATE and laughed and talked about the wedding—the highlights, the relatives who had embarrassed themselves, the plans they'd all made with the guests who were still in town.

The food was good, and everyone was happy and relaxed. Martina thought about how it felt to have everyone she loved together in the same room—including Chris. He hadn't fit in with her family before—not really. But he was fitting in now. Something had changed. Something that mattered. He was talking and laughing with everyone as though he belonged here.

Which, to her, he did.

When breakfast was over, Patrick and Sofia went into their room to get ready for their honeymoon trip to Paris—which Patrick's parents were paying for, and which Martina tried not to be bitterly jealous about. Chris and Benny sat on the sofa talking about something, while TJ took the baby into a back bedroom to change him.

Martina and Bianca cleared the table and started cleaning up in the kitchen, putting away food and stacking dishes in the dishwasher.

"So, what happened?" Bianca asked in a low tone so the others wouldn't hear. "I thought you two had a fight yesterday in the vine-yard. Then you left ... and this morning you show up looking like you've had the best sex of your life."

"I did have the best sex of my life."

"Well, congratulations. But how did you get from yelling in the grapevines to this? And where do things stand now?" Bianca stood with one fist on her hip, a dish towel clasped in one hand.

Martina couldn't keep the goofy smile off her face. "Now ... we're in love. And he wants to want to have kids."

"He wants to want them."

"Yes. All of this is about his past, Bianca. And he's working with a therapist. For me. Because he wants to be healthy for me."

"Well, that's really something." Bianca looked impressed. "I mean ... you know it's no guarantee though, right? Even with a therapist, he might not resolve everything. It's not that easy. It's not—"

"I know, Bianca. Don't ruin this for me. I'm happy. And we're not rushing things. It'll take as long as it takes."

"Then I'm happy for you." Bianca reached out and pulled Martina into a tight hug.

"I'm happy for me, too."

WHILE MARTINA and Bianca talked about that, Chris talked to Benny about something else.

"I've been thinking about that app you suggested."

"What app?" She looked as though she had no idea what he was talking about.

"The app to teach people marine biology. Remember? You pitched it to me at the restaurant?"

Benny let out a guffaw. "That was just a ploy to get you together with Martina. I thought you understood that."

"I did. I do. But that doesn't make it a bad idea."

Her eyes widened. "Really?"

"Sure. We could design it for schoolkids. They could access free games that incorporate things like the names of sea creatures and facts about ocean ecology and climate change, like that. I'd need you for the details on that end of it."

"Huh. A free app? But how would you pay for it? That's—"

"Ads. In-app purchases. Upgrades. Leave that part to me. That's kind of my thing."

"But ..."

"If you're interested, we'll talk."

"Hell yes, I'm interested."

"Good." He grinned, pleased. "I'll have my people call your people."

She looked flustered. "I ... But ..."

"Benny, that last part was a joke."

"Oh. Ha, ha. You don't have people."

"Of course I have people. But I'm assuming you don't, so ..."

"Asshole." But she said it fondly, with a grin.

AFTER MARTINA CLOSED escrow on the Lodge Hill property, she and Chris celebrated with a glass of wine at Fermentations on Main Street.

"I'm so excited," she told him. "I can't wait to start planning the renovations."

He started to say something about helping, and she cut him off. "I *don't* want you to help me pay for them."

"I wasn't going to say that."

"You weren't?"

"No."

She took a sip of her wine—an excellent chardonnay—and put the glass back on the table. "Then what?"

"I was going to say we could do some of the work ourselves. You know, get in there with hammers and power tools ..."

"Really? You're kidding. You couldn't even get your car door put back together."

"It's done. You haven't been out to the garage lately, but ... the door's great. It's perfect."

"You're kidding," she said again.

"Nope."

"So, you broke down and paid someone to do it, then?" Martina tried to sound nonjudgmental.

"No. I paid someone to *show* me how to do it, then I did it myself." He grinned at her, and the grin—the sheer happiness behind it— made her smile, too. "I figure that's fair game, right?"

"Sure. That's fair game."

"So, I can pay someone to teach me how to work on the house. That guy Noah, maybe ..."

"I'm sure he'd be happy to."

"I know you wanted to do it yourself, with nobody's help. So if that's stepping over a line ..."

"Writing a check would be stepping over a line. Helping me hammer nails is something different. After all, it's going to be our house someday, not just mine. At least, that's what I'm hoping."

"Me too." Chris nodded, clearly pleased with himself.

"You'd really do that for me? I mean, put on some jeans and work boots and get out there with a hammer and all that?"

"I'd do that and more. I love you, Martina."

"I love you, too."

They kissed, and he tasted like a spicy, peppery cabernet sauvignon.

"I think this is going to work," she said.

They both understood she wasn't just talking about rebuilding a house. She was talking about building a life.

"I think I should take you home so we can seal the deal the right way." He kissed her deeply enough that other patrons in the tasting room were starting to notice.

"Which home? Yours or mine?"

"Wherever you are is home, Martina."

"Talk like that will get you everything."

That's what he was counting on.

• • •

To see where the character Christopher Mills started, and to read about the incident that almost destroyed his friendship with Will Bachman, read *Nearly Wild*, the third book in the Main Street Merchants series. Learn more at www.lindaseed.com.